Project Governance

RALF MÜLLER
PM Concepts, Sweden

Routledge
Taylor & Francis Group

LONDON AND NEW YORK

First published 2009 by Gower Publishing

Published 2016 by Routledge
2 Park Square, Milton Park, Abingdon, Oxon OX14 4RN
711 Third Avenue, New York, NY 10017, USA

Routledge is an imprint of the Taylor & Francis Group, an informa business

British Library Cataloguing in Publication Data
Müller, Ralf
   Project governance. - (Fundamentals of project management)
   1. Project management 2. Corporate governance
   I. Title II. Series
658.4'04-dc22

Library of Congress Cataloging-in-Publication Data
Müller, Ralf.
   Project governance / by Ralf Müller.
     p. cm. -- (Fundamentals of project management)
   Includes bibliographical references and index.
   ISBN 978-0-566-08866-7
   1. Project management. I. Title.
HD69.P75.M855 2009
658.4'04--dc22

                                                                                    2008050385

ISBN 13: 978-0-566-08866-7 (pbk)

CONTENTS

LIST OF FIGURES

LIST OF TABLES

ACKNOWLEDGEMENTS

I am grateful to several people for their help and support in writing this book.

I should give particular mention to David Keech. He read each chapter of the book at least twice and made a large number of comments. Following his input the text became much more readable and structured. Through his input the text remained aligned with a practitioner's view of the subject. His contributions to the practical application of this book were substantial.

I should further mention my wife Renate, who proofread the draft and provided me with an outsider's view on the text.

Finally, large parts of the text are based on research studies I carried out over the last decade. These studies were done with a number of researchers whose work and experience provided me with lots of insight into the research areas and made this book possible.

CHAPTER 1

INTRODUCTION

Interest in governance is growing rapidly. Well known scandals, such as those at Enron, WorldCom and Societé Generale, made inadequate governance and investor protection a subject of public interest at the turn of the millennium. This led to the refinement of existing governance policies and laws, as well as new developments, such as the Sarbanes-Oxley Act (SOX) in the USA and the Higgs Report in the UK, aiming to prevent similar events in the future. SOX, in particular, aims for early disclosure of possible financial risk, including those related to projects.

Even though governance has become a frequently used term in recent years, it is not a new concept. The term is derived from the Latin word *gubernare* meaning 'to steer'. While originally describing the government of countries, it is nowadays synonymous with the good and transparent management of firms and institutions.

Contemporary governance is grounded in Foucault's (1926–1984) philosophy of Neo-Liberalism, in which individuals are not directly 'steered' by their supervisors (for example, state government), but through subtle forces in the society within which they live. Lemke (2001, p. 201) summarized Foucault's perspective:

> *The Neo-Liberal forms of government [...] characteristically develop indirect techniques for leading and controlling individuals without at the same time being responsible for them. The strategy of rendering individual subjects 'responsible' [...] entails shifting the responsibility for social risks [...] into the domain for which the individual is responsible and transforming it into a problem of 'self-care'.*

Governance is thus about 'the conduct of conduct', shaped by self-regulating relationships among the forces within a society. This leads to the development of laws and contextual frameworks which shape, but do not necessarily determine every action of the members of a society (Clegg 1994, Clegg et al. 2002). To that end *governance is ultimately concerned with creating the conditions for ordered rule and collective action* (Stoker 1998, p. 155). Thus governance within organizations is a form of self regulation where the regulator is part of the system under regulation.

The related Governance Theory was originally developed from policy research in political science. It has outgrown its initial context and is nowadays applied in different sectors of industry, for example, within construction and IT (Pryke 2005, Niehaves, Klose and Becker 2006 respectively). Governance Theory refers to two main components:

- *Actors*, with their individual perspectives and meanings, who act within the system, but collectively can regulate or counter-regulate the system.
- *Institutions* (often in the form of rules), which shape the context within which actors' behaviour occurs.

Accordingly, governance theory addresses the overlap in responsibilities between regulating body and regulated member.

Governance, applied at the corporate level, affects projects through its impact on the behaviour of people. Thus it needs to be implemented through a framework that guides managers in their daily work of decision making and action taking. In projects governance implementation is often defined in terms of policies, processes, roles and responsibilities. This allows for a smooth integration between organization-wide, general processes and the specific sub-processes related to projects.

WHAT IS GOVERNANCE AND WHY DO WE NEED IT?

Governance provides a framework for ethical decision making and managerial action within an organization that is based on transparency, accountability and defined roles. It also provides a clear distinction between *ownership* and *control* of tasks. It sets the boundaries for management action, by defining the goals of the organization and the means by which they should be attained, as well as the processes that managers should use to run their areas of responsibility. Without a governance structure, an organization runs the risk of conflicts and inconsistencies between the various means of achieving organizational goals, the processes and resources, thereby causing costly inefficiencies that impact negatively on both smooth running and bottom line profitability.

DEFINITIONS

Throughout this book the word *organization* is used as a generic term for various levels of the corporate hierarchy. Specifically organization can refer to:

- The corporation itself.
- A division with the corporation.

- A department within the division.
- Work groups and other dynamic organizations.
- Temporary organizations that are projects.
- Any other organizational structure as defined by the corporation.

In most cases, the governance principles covered in this book can apply to any or all levels of that hierarchy. In cases where the entireties of all organizational entities are addressed the more specific term, firm or corporation is used.

From the widespread use of the term governance and its application in, for example, politics, industry and education, a number of definitions have emerged: They range from narrow and specific to broad and general definitions of governance. Among the narrow definitions are those developed from a traditional financial perspective, which limits governance to the relationship between a company and its shareholders, thereby ignoring the interests of other stakeholders. This is often explained in terms of Shareholder Theory and Agency Theory, which is described below. Among the broader and more general definitions is the early definition of corporate governance by OECD (2004):

> *Corporate governance involves a set of relationships between a company's management, its board, its shareholders and other stakeholders. Corporate governance also provides the structure through which the objectives of the company are set, and the means of attaining those objectives and monitoring performance are determined.*

This definition of corporate governance takes a wider spectrum of stakeholders into account, such as employees, customers and suppliers. This definition is often seen as related to stakeholder theory.

In any of these definitions governance regulates the methods and processes of:

- *Defining the objectives of an organization.* This often derives from the strategy of an organization, or the specific contribution an organization can provide to achieve the strategic objectives of a corporation.
- *Providing the means to achieve those objectives.* This addresses the provision of requisite resources (in form of human resources, budget, time and so on) for the members of an organization to enable them to carry out their responsibilities.
- *Controlling progress.* This addresses the need for supervision to control the appropriate use of the resources provided; the application of appropriate processes, tools, techniques and quality standards to create the organization's products or services, as well as checking the need or marketability of the organization's products and services over time.

These three components of governance are not limited to the top of the organizational hierarchy. They are addressed at every level in an organization. While broadest in scope at the top of the organization, this is broken down to the different management functions, horizontally and vertically along the organizational hierarchy. Thus, the need for governance emerges at every node of a management hierarchy within an organization. It constitutes the overall framework for management decision making within the organization. Within the scope addressed through this book governance can be defined as:

> *Governance, as it applies to portfolios, programs, projects, and project management, coexists within the corporate governance framework. It comprises the value system, responsibilities, processes and policies that allow projects to achieve organizational objectives and foster implementation that is in the best interests of all the stakeholders, internal and external, and the corporation itself.*

GOVERNANCE THEORIES

Shareholder Theory

The Shareholder Theory of corporate governance assumes that the main purpose of an organization is to maximize shareholder return on investment (ROI). This requires structures (such as contracts, processes and policies) to assure managerial action is always in the best interests of the shareholders. This model is often related to USA and UK based corporate governance approaches. It is strongly expressed in the Chicago School of Law and Economics. Shareholder Theory sees a company as the property of its shareholders. Managers (including board of directors) are seen as agents of the shareholders (Clarke, 2004). So the relationship between managers and shareholders is explained by Agency Theory.

This implies an organizational value system which prioritizes the interests of shareholders over those of other stakeholders, resulting in a narrow focus on quantitative financial results measures at the expense of more qualitative objectives, such as employee well-being, ethical standards and good relationships with the society in which the corporation exists. Proponents of this governance approach often refer to the difficulties in managing a diverse set of stakeholders in alternative governance structures and the need to focus managers' attention towards a single bottom-line result.

In project-oriented organizations, portfolio managers often act in the best interest of the shareholders of a company, thus take a shareholder perspective when deciding on whether or not to take on projects (Blomquist and Müller 2006). This is supported by Turner (1998a, 1998b), who showed the influence of individual projects on shareholder value:

> *Projects are undertaken to add value to the sponsoring organisation. In the private sector this ultimately means increasing the value of shares to the holders of equity in the company.*

However, research by Cooper, Edgett and Kleinschmidt (2004a, 2004b and 2004c) on portfolio management approaches and company results showed that companies trying to optimize their project portfolio mainly by maximizing financial returns are among the worst in their industry. Causality, however, is not yet researched. It remains unclear whether the poor performance of such companies is caused by their narrow focus on financial results, or whether an already existing poor performance causes this prioritization on financial measures.

Stakeholder Theory

Stakeholder Theory takes the wider social responsibility of organizations into account. In Stakeholder Theory a firm is a system of stakeholders, which operates within the wider host society, which, in turn, provides the legal and market infrastructure for the firm's activities. The purpose of the firm is to create wealth and value for its stakeholders (Clarke 2004).

Stakeholder Theory suggests that an organization's objectives should be developed by balancing the conflicting interests and claims of the different stakeholders, such as managers, employees, suppliers and the wider society. Objectives under Stakeholder Theory include traditional financial objectives (that is, Return on Assets (RoA), Return on Sales (RoS), Revenue growth and so on.) over an extended period of time, such as five years. In addition, corporate social performance measures such as the organization's reputation, the organization's attractiveness as an employer and generation of good-will from the society in which it operates are also important. This contrasts with companies run under Shareholder Theory which usually focus on short term financial results.

Stakeholders are defined as all those who have a stake in the organization; that is, something to gain or lose through the actions of the organization. The definitions range from narrow perspectives, which only include a few closely linked groups, such as employees and suppliers, to wider definitions, which include communities, industries and society. In recent years the latter has emerged amongst business and management schools as Corporate Social Responsibility (CSR).

Stakeholder approaches include taking into account the quality of relationships between the organization and its employees, suppliers, clients and society at large, as well as the balancing of financial gains among internal stakeholders (for example, employees and managers) and external stakeholders (for example, shareholders and community). Proponents of the Stakeholder Theory of Governance claim that this approach allows for coordination of corporate knowledge and activities across the boundaries of individual companies to achieve concerted productivity gains. A typical example is the emergence of Silicon Valley as a combination of knowledge and productivity, based on attractiveness through technological cross-fertilization and mutual gains in form of good relationships and employee stock options (Clarke 2004).

Organizations are not always at one of the ends of the spectrum, but are at a position that allows identifying their preference for greater *shareholder* or greater *stakeholder* orientation. Thus, organizations execute their programs and projects within this spectrum of shareholder to stakeholder perspective, depending on the corporation's governance philosophy. The associated governance theories for projects are Transaction Costs Economics (TCE) and Agency Theory. Here TCE applies especially to the early (pre-contract) phases of a project, where the contract type and governance structure of the project are developed. Agency Theory applies more to the later (post-contract) phases of projects, where information imbalance between Project Owner and Project Manager can create the principal-agent problem (Müller and Turner 2005). Both theories are briefly addressed in the following.

Transaction Costs Economics (TCE)

TCE originated in economics and can be loosely characterized by the classic *make or buy* decision. It is used to justify a decision to make a product internally or to buy it from the open marketplace. The pros and cons are shown in Table 1.1 below:

Table 1.1   Pros and cons of make or buy decision

	MAKE	BUY
Pros	Better control of fit for purpose Maladaptation costs are minimized	Lower prices through economies of scale and price competition in the marketplace
Cons	Higher cost	Adaptation costs higher

TCE focuses on the individual transaction which converts input to desired output. According to Williamson (1975) the make or buy decision is based on a combination of:

- The degree of *asset specificity* as the main influential factor. This is the extent to which the object of the transaction is specific (or unique) to the individual transaction and can not be redeployed in future transactions.
- The degree of *uncertainty* which arises from:
  - a lack of communication or conscious supply of false and misleading signals;
  - the general uncertainty in human behaviour;
  - the general risk of the undertaking.
- The *frequency* of the transaction. TCE was originally developed for repetitive, routine transactions undertaken by the classical organization, managed rigidly by functional and hierarchical structures. Within these repetitive transactions no specialized governance structures are required, whereas highly unique transactions demand specific governance structures.

TCE '*regards a firm as a governance structure, rather than a production function*' (Williamson 1985, p. 387). The associated costs for governing these transactions vary because:

> *Transaction costs are economized by assigning transactions (which differ in their attributes) to governance structures (the adaptive capacities and associated costs of which differ) in a discriminating way* (Williamson 1985, p. 18).

TCE implies that organizations adapt their governance structures to achieve the lowest possible transaction costs. Transaction costs are the economic equivalent to friction in physical systems, stemming from the complexity of the relationship between buyer and seller and the impossibility of developing and agreeing contracts comprehensive enough to cover all eventualities in the transaction. To economize on transaction costs TCE proposes that high levels of asset specificity, uncertainty and contract incompleteness lead to *make* decisions, whereas low levels lead to *buy* decisions (Adler et al. 1998).

TCE is criticized for the crudeness of its primitive models, underdeveloped tradeoffs, severe measurement problems and too many degrees of freedom (Williamson 1985). However, as a theory developed in marketing it is frequently used to explain marketing phenomena, such as joint projects between independent firms in a buyer – seller relationship.

In projects, TCE explains the need for different governance structures for different projects along the need for different contracts when either buying a product in the market or making it within the organization. A fix-price, fix-date delivery contract for a project or components thereof requires different governance and control structures than a time and material or cost reimbursement contract.

Agency Theory

Agency Theory relates to the shareholder theory of the organization. It addresses the potential for conflict of interest that arises between shareholders and managers of a firm through the definition of a principal–agent relationship between these parties. The potential for principal–agent problems arises when one party (the principal, that is, the shareholder) depends on another party (the agent, that is, the manager) to undertake some action on the principal's behalf (Bergen et al. 1992, Jensen 2000). The delegation of decision-making authority from principle to agent can cause problems because:

- the interests of principal and agent will typically diverge if both are trying to maximize their individual gains or utility in the relationship;
- the principal cannot perfectly and without cost monitor the actions of the agent;
- the principal cannot perfectly and without cost monitor and acquire the information available to or possessed by the agent (Barney and Hesterly 1996, Jensen 2000).

These problems are summarized in the two Agency problems, these are:

- Information imbalances between principal and agent during the *pre-contractual phase*, when the principal selects and offers a contract to a possible agent. Here the principal is assumed to know more about the nature of the task the agent should perform as well as the personal characteristic needed to perform this task. This is often referred to as *ex ante*, or adverse selection problem.
- Information asymmetries during the post-contractual stage, caused by incomplete information on the side of the principal about the agent's actions while carrying out the assigned task, as well as the agent's higher level of task related information arising from closer involvement in day-to-day activities. This is often referred to as the *ex post*, or moral hazard problem.

These problems are addressed in Agency Theory by attempting to realign the interests of the principal and agent through effective use of contracts. By defining either actual behaviour of agents or the outcomes of agents' tasks, contracts ensure that actions regarded as most appropriate by the principal yield the highest payoff for the agent (Bergen et al. 1992).

Agency Theory has been criticized for taking an inherent investor view only and for assuming that humans are primarily motivated by financial gain. However, *'empirical evidence is on balance supportive of agency theory'* (Barney and Hesterly 1996, p. 128).

The above mentioned principal–agent problems are equally applicable at the project level, with the project sponsor as principal and the project manager as agent.

The theoretical framework outlined above addressed the continuum of corporate level governance theories (from shareholder to stakeholder) within which the related project level governance theories (principal–agent and TCE) reside.

GOVERNANCE OF PROJECTS AND PROJECT MANAGEMENT AS A SUBSET OF CORPORATE GOVERNANCE

Governance is not confined to the board level of the organization. Many of the major project failures were caused by lack of appropriate governance at the level of individual projects and their management. Companies with a large percentage of their business done through projects are especially dependent on good project results. In these organizations, the impact of project results on corporate results demands rigid governance structures for projects and their management. Project management methodologies, such as PRINCE2 (OGC 2008) suggest that governance of projects and project management originates at the top of the organization and trickles down to the lower levels.

At the corporate level, governance of projects and project management is a responsibility of the board of directors, including:

- Definition and goal setting for the projects, programs and portfolios of the organization, in order to achieve its strategic objectives.
- Definition of the means to achieve these objectives through:
  - Defining the model by which projects, programs and portfolios will be governed, including the means of prioritizing scarce resources amongst projects competing for those resources. This constitutes governance of projects.
  - Developing enterprise project management capabilities to ensure projects, programs and portfolios can be successfully implemented, including the possible establishment of project management offices. This constitutes governance of project management (Crawford and Turner 2005).
- Controlling progress in the implementation of these actions and taking corrective actions in case of plan deviation.

This structure includes a governance entity at the level of projects, programs and portfolios. At the portfolio level it is the board of directors which defines portfolio goals as a subset of the organization's strategic goals, the criteria for prioritization and measurement of progress and the means to monitor progress.

At the level of individual projects and programs it is the Sponsor or Project/ Program Steering Group that sets the business objective and agrees the program/ project deliverables, provides the means (resources, facilities, processes, project manager and so on) to achieve objectives and defines the means to control progress (for example, at milestones and Stage Gate Reviews).

PARADIGMS FOR PROJECT AND PROJECT MANAGEMENT GOVERNANCE

Research has shown that organizations differ in the priorities they assign to the project process or the project outcome (for example, Brown and Eisenhardt 1997).

Organizations emphasizing the importance of following a strict project management process to accomplish project outcomes are *behaviour* oriented. These organizations perceive project management as being inherent in the process of delivering the project outcome, often in form of a technology development methodology or a corporate project management methodology. These organizations are ambivalent as to whether project management is done by individuals internal or external to their organization, as long as the process conforms to given standards or policies.

In contrast, organizations emphasizing the fit of the project's deliverables to existing expectations are *outcome* oriented. These organizations give more autonomy to their projects and project managers than behaviour oriented organizations. Typically, they do perceive project management as a corporate core competency and a major differentiator for competing in the marketplace. In these organizations projects are typically managed by dedicated project managers, who possess a wider spectrum of project management related skills and are directly employed by the organization.

The combination of these two approaches with an underlying corporate shareholder or stakeholder philosophy provides four different governance paradigms, shown in Table 1.2.

The *Conformist* paradigm utilizes strict compliance with existing processes, rules and policies to attempt to ensure lowest project costs in environments with a relatively homogeneous set of projects. A typical example is quality improvement projects using Six Sigma techniques. Due to their repetitive nature, strict process

Table 1.2   Four governance paradigms

	Shareholder Orientation	Stakeholder Orientation
Outcome control focus	**Flexible Economist Paradigm** Achieving highest possible Return on Investment (ROI) for the organizations' shareholders through optimization of the management of projects. Done by establishing project management as core competence (for example, through training, certification and related career ladders) executed by professional project managers who are employees of the organization. They are guided by tactical Project Management Offices (PMO), which support and control the application of accepted project management methods and tools.	**Versatile Artist Paradigm** Consists of balancing the qualitative and quantitative requirements of a wide range of stakeholders (both often differ by project). Achieved through selection or tailoring of project management methods for the different projects. Project management is understood to be a core competence of the organization and a profession of the individual. Both aspects are guided by a strategic PMO which defines the organization's business results to be achieved through project management.
Behaviour control focus	**Conformist Paradigm** Maximizing shareholder return by strictly applying existing development methodologies. Project management is often a subset (possibly invisible) in the specific development processes for technical products or services. Project management is understood as an on-the-side task for leading technical experts.	**Agile Pragmatist Paradigm** Balances the diverse requirements of a variety of stakeholders by maximizing their collective benefits through the timely development of functionality or value. Project management methods maximize value of a series of project outcomes over time, based on the strict prioritization of user needs.

orientation and relatively low level of innovation these projects are often led by technical experts or specialists in a given field. Project management is implied in the repetitive execution of the Six Sigma process.

The *Flexible Economist* paradigm aims for low project costs through a well informed selection of project management methodologies which ensure economic delivery by marginally compromising other success criteria. The assumption underlying this paradigm is that well educated and experienced project managers will identify the process that will deliver the most economic result and save costs through professional management of the project. Skilled, educated, flexible and experienced project managers are needed to economize on methods in environments with a relatively heterogeneous set of projects. Examples include customer specific software application development projects in fixed price contracts.

The *Versatile Artist* paradigm aims at maximizing benefits through balancing the diverse set of requirements arising from a number of different stakeholders and their particular needs and desires. Balance is achieved either by tailoring existing project management methodologies or by developing new ones to balance these diverse requirements. The assumption underlying this paradigm is that versatile and experienced project managers can balance diverse and often conflicting requirements, such as those for low costs at highest quality from customers, as well as attractiveness as employer and high productivity from internal management. Examples of organizations using this governance paradigm include project management consulting companies, which work with very heterogeneous sets of projects in high technology or high risk environments. Flexible and creative approaches to project management are required, with little room for error.

The *Agile Pragmatist* paradigm aims for maximization of technical usability, often through a time-phased approach to the development and product release of functionality over a period of time. The assumptions underlying this paradigm are that a limited but key functionality (especially in software development) allows for a limited but early use of the new product. Products developed under this paradigm grow from a core functionality, which is developed first, to ever increasing features, which although of a lesser and lesser importance to the core functionality, enhance the product in flexibility, sophistication and ease-of-use. Examples include projects for IT software development, where a few key functions allow a limited productive use of the product. Or software release updates, where new and improved functionality must be prioritized by the users and the time of product release is linked with a longer term release roadmap. These projects often use Agile methods, such as Scrum, to identify project scope to be achieved using the sponsor's prioritization of functions over a given timeframe.

Larger and complex enterprises apply different governance paradigms in different parts of their organization, often reflecting the strategic goals, preferences of the leaders, market demands and the idiosyncratic level of project management maturity of a particular part of an organization.

The choice of governance paradigm impacts the breadth and depth with which governance of projects and project management is implemented in an organization. In the following chapters of this book, the implications on how-to-govern arising from the different paradigms are discussed.

This chapter introduced corporate governance, its underlying philosophy, definitions and theories. By linking corporate governance theory to governance theories in a project based environment, a theoretical framework has been developed consisting of four different paradigms for governance of projects and their management.

The next chapter starts by looking at projects as temporary organizations and the related governance processes. Then governance of project management is addressed by looking at existing guidelines and practices.

CHAPTER 2

OBJECTIVES AND INSTITUTIONS

This chapter introduces the need for and objectives of, governance of projects as temporary organizations. It examines the governance institutions required together with their respective roles and responsibilities. Finally, three existing governance standards are summarized and how they need to be applied with a different perspective to governance of projects and project management.

PROJECTS AS TEMPORARY ORGANIZATIONS

Projects are created to accomplish an organization's strategy. Figure 2.1 shows the relationship between organizational strategy and associated projects. It shows how strategy and projects are linked through a delivery circle and a control circle.

The delivery circle is shown by solid arrows. Strategy determines the strategic goals necessary, which, in turn, determine the goals of the project portfolios, as well as the projects and programs required within the portfolio, each governed by their respective Steering Group. These groups own the business case. The business case stems from the organization's strategy and determines the scope of individual projects and programs which are set up to contribute to the achievement of these strategic goals.

The control circle is shown by dotted line arrows. Project Management Offices (or similar control structures) enable control of the alignment between strategy and capabilities via information flow from projects to the various governance levels in the organization (Hobbs and Aubry 2007). For example, the Project Management Office (PMO) aggregates project performance information for the portfolio manager, who takes this information into account for future portfolio decisions. The portfolio manager then reports performance data to senior management enabling them to refine or adjust the organization's strategy as appropriate according to the organization's capabilities.

The heart of each project is a task (or endeavour) to create an outcome. This outcome needs to be accomplished by people, within the boundaries of time, cost and other constraints. Therefore a project can be considered to be an organization

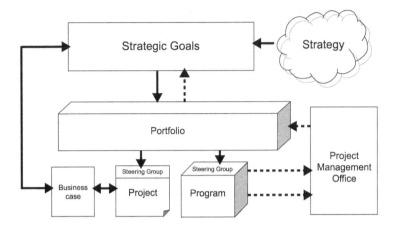

Figure 2.1   The relationship between strategy and projects

of people for the accomplishment of a specific outcome, with a planned start date, end date and associated constraints. A project is a temporary organization due to its planned start and end date. Projects reside within the permanent organization. That is the corporation itself, a permanent organization with no planned end date.

When Rodney Turner and I looked at projects from a corporate perspective, we identified projects as a production function of the firm. Here individual projects serve as agencies to manage uncertainties in new undertakings, stimulate change of different kinds and utilize resources. Within each agency the project manager acts as CEO of this temporary organization (Turner and Müller 2003). All these agency functions and agency decisions need to be aligned continuously with the firm's strategy and its tactical objectives and capabilities. Therefore the need arises for governance as a framework for decision making in and for projects. Just as the permanent organization needs governance, so does the temporary organization that is a project.

Aims, purpose and objectives in the governance of projects and project management

Given the need for governance of temporary organizations, what should the aims and objectives be? The overriding aim of project governance is a consistent and predictable delivery of projects and programs in accordance with their planned contribution to corporate strategy and stakeholder expectations. This is achieved through a consistent and coherent execution of governance roles and responsibilities by the various management levels throughout the organization. These roles and responsibilities are examined in the following sections of this book.

The purpose of governance structures is the alignment of the objectives at the different management levels of the organization in order to allow for most effective and efficient project planning and execution, within the boundaries of corporate governance.

Objectives of project governance include:

*   Fostering of an environment allowing projects to be successful.
*   Prioritization of projects for best use of resources.
*   Identification of projects in trouble. Rescue, suspension or termination of these projects as appropriate.

Governance then, defines the processes, roles and accountabilities of the managers in the different institutions which perform corporate governance. The governance institutions, presented in the following section, need to collaborate for successful project work.

INSTITUTIONS RESPONSIBLE FOR GOVERNANCE OF PROJECTS AND PROJECT MANAGEMENT

Board of Directors

This is the highest level of management in the corporation and governance originates at this level. Directors must find the appropriate balance between governance of projects and governance of project management. While the former comprises the extent to which the business is run through the use of projects, the latter addresses the capacity and capabilities of project and program managers needed to execute these projects. Here the foundation is laid for the governance paradigm to be used throughout the entire organization (see Table 1.1).

Project governance decisions made by the board of directors include strategy formulation, which decides on the types, quantities and scope of the various projects needed to implement the strategy; for example, a strategy to spend 50 per cent of the annual budget for revenue generating projects, 30 per cent for Research and Development (R&D) projects, 10 per cent on quality improvement (including employee training) and an expected 10 per cent on legally enforced *must-do* projects. These numbers (and their variation from prior year) give the first indication about the number and type of projects to be expected. This information is then taken up by the portfolio managers to make decisions on which projects to accept into the portfolio and which to start, suspend, continue or terminate.

Project management governance decisions include fundamental questions on the strategic value of project management to the organization. Is project management to be done *on the side* by technical specialists who have little or no training or previous experience of project management, by temporarily contracted external project managers, or by full-time professional project managers employed by the organization? These decisions are often made on an ad-hoc or unconscious basis. However, these decisions are Project Management Governance decisions and need to be made as part of a conscious overall strategy. Decisions to be made include the quantity and quality of:

- portfolio management personnel;
- project and program sponsors including steering groups;
- program and project managers;
- possible Project/Program Management Office (PMO) functions;
- communication structures, such as reporting and disclosure at the project, program, PMO and portfolio level.

It is fundamental that the board of directors decides on the quantities of these roles and the skills and experience levels required for each. The more subtle project management governance decisions may not be made as clearly and consciously. These consist of defining the associated authorities and accountabilities for each role and linking them into an overall project and project management governance process for the organization. This is then often formulated as policy and made available to all managers.

The governance paradigm established through the board's decisions on the above items is then filtered down the organization. Governance of individual projects is done mainly through portfolio managers, sponsors/steering groups and strategic PMOs. Implementation of the policy and actual governance of project management is mainly undertaken by middle management and tactical PMOs.

INSTITUTIONS FOR GOVERNANCE OF PROJECTS

Within the given governance paradigm and the decisions made by the board of directors, the project governance institutions decide on the priority of individual projects and also the project management processes, techniques, acceptance criteria, type of project management skills and so on needed at the project level.

Portfolio management

A project portfolio is a grouping of projects around a particular skill set needed for executing these projects. The projects in any individual portfolio do not necessarily have to be related to each other. However, the requisite skills sets (or resources) do have to be. Large organizations often run several portfolios in parallel; for example, one portfolio of application development projects for external customers in the banking industry, another for retail solutions for external customers, a third for internal IT projects.

Project governance decisions made at the portfolio level are:

- acceptance of projects into the portfolio, based on the organization's strategy, the portfolio optimization strategy and the organization's capabilities;
- prioritizing of projects, including start, end, suspension and termination of projects;
- allocation of resources to projects based on project priorities;
- identification of skills bottlenecks or other strategic resources, which risk delays in delivery of projects within the portfolio;
- possible remedies and mitigation strategies for any risks, issues and so on encountered within the portfolio.

Publications like the *PMI® Practice Standard for Project Portfolio Management* (PMI 2006a) by the Project Management Institute (PMI)[1] describe the process and techniques for selecting and prioritizing projects in a portfolio. They are increasingly used by organizations to define their portfolio management approach.

Sponsors and steering groups

A sponsor is usually a manager whose organization provides funding for the project. It is anticipated that this organization receives the most benefits from the project outcome. The sponsor is therefore the person most interested in the success of the project.

Occasionally this function is separated into a project owner who receives the benefits of the project outcome and a project sponsor organization which provides the budget for the project. An example is an international development project where a local government owns a project and the funding comes from World Bank.

Steering Groups are committees set up to implement governance of the project. They are also known as Steering Committees or Project Boards. They are typically chaired by the sponsor. PRINCE2 (CCTA 2000) suggests that steering groups consist of, as a minimum:

- The project sponsor: the manager who orders the project and expects to gain the majority of the benefits from the outcome of the project. This is

---

1   PMI is a registered trademark and service mark of the Project Management Institute, Inc.

often, but not always, the same manager or organization that provides the funding for the project.

- The project manager: the manager who is given the responsibility for the day-to-day management of the project on behalf of the steering group. The project manager has a role in the steering group and will often attend many steering group meetings, but is not a member of it.

Beyond the minimum (above), typical additional members of the steering group are:

- Managers representing the users of the project outcome.
- The major suppliers and stakeholder groups.
- Executive management.
- Others on demand. These may often be temporary additions to the core steering group members. In such cases they may have a specific role to play, such as SME (Subject Matter Expert) manager for a particular phase of the project and are no longer required once that particular phase has been completed.

Sponsored projects are selected by portfolio management for execution. Once selected, either an individual sponsor, or a steering group is formally assigned ownership. The sponsor then owns the business case for this project and is accountable to senior management for achievement of the business goals associated with it. In most projects the sponsor is the chairperson of the steering group. This practice is very common in industrial and technical projects where the sponsor's role is more closely related to the conceptualization and realization of the business case and benefits. In contrast, the rest of the steering group tends to be slightly more concerned with the governance of project execution.

Steering groups are ultimately responsible for project success and constitute the governance institution closest to project execution. They appoint the project manager, set the parameters in terms of budget, time, success criteria (for example, quality levels) and define the goals to be achieved within these limits. The sponsor and/or steering group then executes governance by providing resources, controlling the project (typically through use of plans), milestones, deliverables and change control and acceptance of project end. In addition they provide advice and guidance as needed to the project manager. During the project's existence the project manager reports to the assigned steering group.

Program management

Programs are groupings of projects with a common goal. Governance comprises determining the framework for management of the projects within the program. This includes, for example, the methodologies to be used, the change management processes to be followed, the type of risk management to be undertaken and the quantity and quality of reporting by each project manager. Program managers act as sponsors for the projects within their program. They are ultimately responsible for achievement of the objectives of all individual projects within the program. An additional program board might be established to take on the steering group function for the entire program, which is then accountable for the achievement of the benefits of the entire program.

Strategic project management offices

The governance institutions described above are either explicitly identifiable within the organization (there are defined roles for portfolio manager and project sponsor), or are more implicit in other management roles such as those of Vice Presidents or heads of R&D departments. However, governance, either explicit or implicit, is always done within in the organization. Someone will decide which projects to accept and which ones to drop.

This is not the case when it comes to Program Management Offices (PMOs). Not all organizations have a PMO, even though PMOs have become very popular in recent years. A wide variety of different types of PMO exists, from the enterprise-wide and strategic to the operational and tactical (Hobbs and Aubry 2007).

The Strategic PMO sets the goals to be achieved in terms of project management results. Typical objectives set by this type of PMO include Corporate Balanced Scorecard measures, such as 'number of red projects', or 'revenue at risk due to red customer delivery projects'. The classification of projects by colour is typically defined along the following lines:

- Green: overall status OK.
- Yellow: plan deviation, project in need of management attention.
- Red: serious deviation from plan, project in danger of failure.

The means to achieve project goals are provided by a tactical PMO, described in the next section. Progress control is done by collecting performance data on all projects in a portfolio. Centralized tools are used for collection of performance data and subsequent classification of projects as red, yellow or green. These data are aggregated into an overall portfolio report for the portfolio manager, which serves as an input to further portfolio decisions and for measuring the portfolio's contribution to corporate strategic objectives.

INSTITUTIONS FOR GOVERNANCE OF PROJECT MANAGEMENT

Using the governance paradigm and decisions made by the board of directors, this group of organizational entities decides on the project management related skill levels required, the depth to which each is required and the quantities needed.

Middle management

Middle managers are responsible for the operational implementation of corporate strategy. This is done via ongoing processes and also projects. For projects middle managers need to recruit, train and maintain a pool of project managers with the level of project management skills required to implement the specific mix of projects used in their organization. Decisions made by middle managers include:

- How many different project management skills levels are needed for the projects in the part of the organization the manager is responsible for.
- What are the particular profiles of the different skills sets needed (for example, junior, experienced and senior project managers).
- What are appropriate training and certification programs for these levels.
- How many project managers are needed for each skill level.

Middle management is ultimately responsible for building up a pool of project managers consisting of people with the specific skill sets required to staff the particular mix of projects in their organization most effectively.

Tactical PMOs

Tactical PMOs work with project managers to ensure each project uses the optimal depth and breadth of methodologies, processes, techniques, tools and other management functions. Therefore tactical PMOs often provide training and consulting services to project managers (Englund and Müller 2005). Even though originally founded to support the Conformist governance paradigm by ensuring better project outcomes, their work has contributed in the long term to the improvement of project managers' skills and fostered a move towards the Flexible Economist governance paradigm.

Questions addressed at the level of the tactical PMO include:

- Which methods, tools, techniques and so on should be used for the different projects in the organization?
- Which areas of project management should be improved within the organization?

- How do we ensure use of appropriate methods, tools and techniques in the project management community within the organization?
- How do we ensure a seamless information flow among and between the different governance institutions (described above)?

Tactical PMOs, even though not present in all organizations, are an important governance institution for quality in project management execution. They have insight into the variety of projects in an organization and the strengths and weaknesses in execution of these projects. That insight enables them to provide training or other practice improvements with a high return on investment.

Now that the institutions have been presented, we can turn our attention to the existing standards and guidelines for governance of projects and project management.

EXISTING STANDARDS AND GUIDELINES

There are four groups of guidelines available:

1. Those developed and marketed by individual consulting firms.
2. Those developed internally by organizations.
3. Those developed by professional organizations.
4. Those developed by governmental organizations.

Most guidelines in the first and second group include subsets of the third and fourth group. Three representatives of the latter two categories are examined below as examples of the difference in perspective they take towards governance.

In the list above, I have excluded governance guidelines for specific industries, such ITIL or CoBiT for management of IT operations. These are not general purpose guidelines for governance of and relating to project management. They mainly address governance from an operational (not project) perspective.

The APM Guide to Governance of Project Management

The *Association for Project Management's* (APM) booklet '*Directing Change: A Guide to Governance of Project Management*' (APM 2004) is developed by a professional organization for project management and belongs to the third category (developed by professional organizations) listed above. It is one of the earliest works on the subject and builds on the OECD definition of governance (see Chapter 1). It defines *Governance of Project Management* as that part of the organizations Corporate Governance that overlaps Project Management. It is written from corporate board of directors' perspective focusing on the board's tasks and responsibilities. The aims include Sarbanes-Oxley (SOX) compliance amongst other topics. Governance of project management is addressed in relation to four main dimensions:

1. *Portfolio direction effectiveness and efficiency*. Ensures that all projects are identified within a portfolio and that the portfolio is consistent with the organization's aims and constraints.
2. *Project sponsorship*. Ensures an effective link between senior executives and project managers by identifying and empowering sponsors with decision making, directing and representational accountabilities.
3. *Project management effectiveness and efficiency*. Ensures that project teams, including the project manager, are well equipped to achieve project objectives. It includes appropriate capabilities, tools and processes, as well as skill and experience of the project managers.
4. *Disclosure and reporting*. Ensures timely availability of relevant and reliable information for the corporation's decision making processes. Requires a culture of open and honest disclosure and may include stakeholders outside the organization.

APM (2004) defines eleven Governance of Project Management Principles (p. 6):

1. The board has overall responsibility for governance of project management.
2. The roles, responsibilities and performance criteria for the governance of project management are clearly defined.
3. Disciplined governance arrangements, supported by appropriate methods and controls, are applied throughout the project life cycle.
4. A coherent and supportive relationship is demonstrated between the overall business strategy and the project portfolio.
5. All projects have an approved plan containing authorization points at which the business case is reviewed and approved. Decisions made at authorization points are recorded and communicated.
6. Members of delegated authorization bodies have sufficient representation, competence, authority and resources to enable them to make appropriate decisions.
7. The project business case is supported by relevant and realistic information that provides a reliable basis for making authorization decisions.
8. The board or its delegated agents decide when independent review of projects and project management systems is required and implement such scrutiny accordingly.
9. There are clearly defined criteria for reporting project status and for the escalation of risks and issues to the levels required by the organization.
10. The organization fosters a culture of improvement and of frank internal disclosure of project information.

11. Project stakeholders are engaged at a level appropriate to their importance to the organization and in a manner that fosters trust.

APM does not promote governance as the strict application of processes and methods, but perceives governance as the flexible and intelligent application of the above principles, together with delegation of responsibility and monitoring of internal control systems.

Tasmanian Government Project Management Guidelines

The following Governance guideline is part of the *Tasmanian Government Project Management Guidelines* (Tasmanian Government 2005). It addresses:

- Objectives of project governance:
  - Planning and managing projects.
  - Achievement of project outcomes with high productivity and quality, at manageable levels of risk.
- Project roles in a project governance structure. At a minimum projects should include people in the following roles:
  - A sponsor: the person responsible and accountable for the project and for securing the project outcome.
  - Business owner(s): the person(s) managing the project outputs after project closure and accountable for the realization of the project outcomes.
  - A project manager: the person managing the project and delivering the outputs.
- Steering Group roles and functions: predominantly as outlined earlier in this chapter.
- Project Management governance models – generic for small to medium, and large and/or complex projects. Guidelines are given for governance models from minimum (for example, sponsor, project manager and quality consultant) to maximum (for example, a complex web of governance institutions).
- Governance of Program Management is described as the application of the governance process, clear roles and steering groups, interlinked and described in a program/project business plan.
- Project Portfolio Management is a formal but dynamic process of accepting and (re-) prioritizing projects to meet business objectives and emerging opportunities.
- The above guidelines are to be accomplished by applying three principles (p. 18):
  - Governance, including roles and responsibilities, is clearly defined, agreed to and signed-off by the Steering Group, as detailed in the Project Business Plan.

- A 'Steering, not Rowing' Group, that is, a group managing at the appropriate level, not at the project level. It is representative of the Project Business Owner(s) and Key Stakeholders, as appropriate.
- Status reporting of project progress takes place tracked against milestones, as outlined in the Project Business Plan. Status reporting also includes identified risks and issues for the project.

For selection of appropriate project managers, the importance of project management skills and experience is outlined specifically for large projects, followed by the need for business knowledge.

OGC Guidelines for Managing Successful Projects (MSP)

The *Office of Government Commerce* (OGC) governance guidelines build on earlier standards such as PRINCE2 (OGC 2008) and are developed by UK government institutions. Similar to the governance guidelines from the Tasmanian Government, the OGC guideline is an extension of an existing methodology for management of projects and programs. Governance is not explicitly addressed, but implicit in the framework for 'Managing Successful Projects' (OGC 2008). The focus is on rigorous and disciplined application of processes, tools and techniques.

MSP is a comprehensive method for management and governance of projects and programs. Governance is addressed at several levels including:

- *Stage Gate Reviews*: Detailed guidance on how to conduct Stage Gate Reviews, questions to ask and decisions to be made.
- *Benefits Management*: Providing process and tools for:
  - Identifying a business idea.
  - Development of a business plan.
  - Project initiation, planning and control.
  - Assessment of benefits achieved.
- *Senior managers*: Outlining senior manager roles in planning and managing successful delivery of projects.

By taking a public procurement perspective in providing in-depth descriptions of processes, tools and techniques needed for management and governance, MSP has become a comprehensive framework for project delivery. MSP covers a wide range of processes, tools, techniques and role descriptions and fosters discipline in their application. However, it does allow for flexibility (for example, add-on of agile capabilities to PRINCE2 through integration of Dynamic Systems Development Method (DSDM)), thus allowing for predictive as well as convergent methods for managing projects.

The three standards presented above show a variety of governance approaches. The Tasmanian Government and OGC approach take a methodology perspective, with the former accentuating the need for Steering Groups and sponsors to 'steer not row' over other approaches and the different skill profiles of projects managers. The latter accentuates stage reviews and project owner responsibilities over the other two governance approaches. APM takes a higher management perspective in a continuously changing business context, by building flexibility in execution, SOX compliance and competence of members of the various governance institutions.

This chapter introduced the need for governance in project-oriented organizations and examined the goals of this governance. The different institutions for governance of projects and project management were introduced. The chapter concluded by looking very briefly at existing standards and identified the differences between them in focus and approach.

The next chapter presents a model for governance of project management.

CHAPTER 3

GOVERNANCE OF PROJECT MANAGEMENT

The previous chapter examined institutions and standards for governance. This chapter introduces a model for governance of project management within companies. It consists of three steps and is suitable for companies with little project work, to companies whose business is based mainly on projects and particularly for the majority of companies who fall between these two extremes.

MIGRATING TO A PROJECT BASED ORGANIZATION

Chapter 2 presented a number of decisions to be made by the board of directors on the quantity and quality of project managers in the corporation. I also discussed the need to establish specific institutions for governance, that is, the awareness of project management at the middle manager level, the building of tactical PMOs, establishment of Steering Groups and so on. I also introduced roles and work of each of these governance institutions within the corporation. The variety of these institutions and their particular roles in governance raises the question of what combination is appropriate for which corporation. Corporations have differing levels of *projectization*; that is, the extent to which their business is based on projects and the degree the project way of working pervades practice within the corporation. A framework is needed to enable corporations to choose their own appropriate governance structure for project management, according to their own level of *projectization*. To develop this framework I will first take a look at the forces that foster good quality in project management delivery and from there develop the steps for economic implementation of governance structures for project management.

Quality of project management

Much has been published and researched on the practices that lead to successful project management. Research has shown that, in summary, there are three forces which impact and determine the quality of project management for any specific project (Müller and Stawicki 2007). These are:

1. *Education*
   'What Can Be Done?'

   The first force is education. Education impacts the skill level and project management knowledge of the project manager. Better educated project managers have a greater repertoire of methods, tools and techniques to manage projects and their inherent management problems. This force determines *what can be done* by the project manager.

2. *Management Demands*
   'What Should Be Done?'

   The second force is management demands. Corporate management determines the extent to which specific project management practices are demanded, for example, by Sponsors, Steering Groups, Program Managers or other line functions supervising the project manager. This force determines how project management should be done by the project manager, for example, which project management methodology to be used, the frequency and contents of status reports and the type of planning and control techniques to be applied. Anything not specifically demanded by management is often neglected by project managers, with an adverse effect on project performance. Management demand determines *what should be done* for good quality project management.

3. *Perceived Economic Pressure*
   'What is Done?'

   The third and most detrimental force is perceived economic pressure. This is the project managers' perception of the economics of the project (for example, costs overruns) and the resulting pressure on them. Project managers with low perceived economic pressure (that is, the project is being successfully managed within the cost and time constraints) tend to have a long-term view of the project, possibly planning follow-on projects. High pressure from steering groups or other stakeholders as a result of plan deviation or unrealistic goals (for example, unrealistic cost and/or time constraints) reduces the time horizon view of the project manager drastically. Being threatened with bad project results and the possibility of being fired, project managers tend to drastically shorten their time horizon when making project decisions. They tend to focus exclusively on their own short-term survival in the current position, with little or no regard to the longer term needs of the organization and the role of the project in meeting them. Emphasizing only short term goals can lead to decisions which are severely detrimental for the project itself, the long-term client relationship and the long-term accomplishments of the organization. This force has a major impact on *what is done* (or *compliance*) by the project manager in a project.

Figure 3.1 shows the related force field analysis. Increasing education and management demand has positive effects on the quality of project management, while the perceived economic pressure has a negative effect.

A framework for organizational migration

Each corporation needs to respond to these three forces with appropriate measures. They need to balance financial investment in project management capabilities against return – that is, measuring Return-on-Investment (ROI) for project management. Corporations whose project-based part of the business is relatively small naturally invest less in project management capabilities. As there are relatively few project improvements in the quality of project management this results in only minor financial gains for the wider organization. In contrast, corporations whose business is almost totally project-based invest much more in their project management capabilities. High quality of project management will result in far more significant financial gains for the wider organization.

Figure 3.2 shows the governance framework as a three-step process. Each step constitutes the equilibrium of the three forces listed above. Migration from step one to step three indicates an increasingly stronger organizational focus on project management capabilities and an associated increase in investment (and potential return) in project management capabilities.

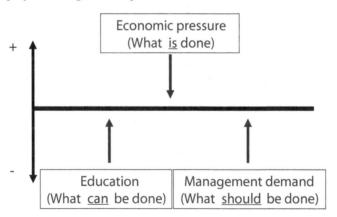

Figure 3.1   Forces impacting quality of project management

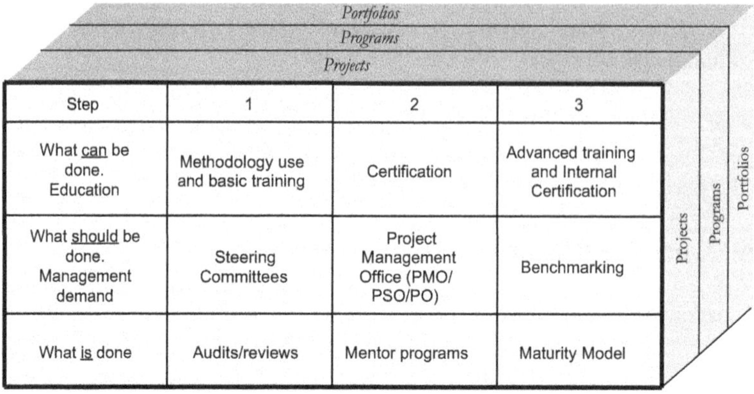

Step	1	2	3
What can be done. Education	Methodology use and basic training	Certification	Advanced training and Internal Certification
What should be done. Management demand	Steering Committees	Project Management Office (PMO/ PSO/PO)	Benchmarking
What is done	Audits/reviews	Mentor programs	Maturity Model

Portfolios
Programs
Projects

Figure 3.2   Governance framework for project management

Primary elements of the framework

Step 1 constitutes the lowest level of investment and return (ROI). This step is indicated when the amount of project-based work is increasing and management has the impression that project results could be improved. The move from zero project management capabilities to those of Step 1 may be inhibited by too strong a focus on the corporation's technical expertise resulting in ignoring possibilities for business improvement. Corporations at Step 1 often use the Conformist or Agile Pragmatist paradigm of governance. At this step project management emerges as a set of procedures extracted from the technical development processes. Figure 3.3 (below) shows the migration.

Step 1 governance measures should be used by all corporations that have at least some project-based work, even those with a minimal project-based work component. Corporations implementing and synchronizing the three measures of Step 1 achieve a good balance between investment in and return on (ROI) project management capability improvement. These corporations may wish to keep their investment in project management governance to this level; higher investment would merely lead to diminishing return (ROI). Corporations with a higher quantity of project-based work may also tend to stay at this step for a while and, following evaluation of the improvements made in terms of project results, move on to step two.

Step 1
At Step 1 corporations implement the following *Education, Management Demand* and *what is done* measures:

1. *Education: Basic Training*
   This may include short project management courses for technical specialists in charge of projects. These people then become the change agents in the corporation by introducing more professional ways of establishing temporary organizations and working within them. This often takes the form of beginning to use project management terminology and introducing a new process for managing projects (using phased approaches and Stage Gate or Milestone/Tollgate models). This fosters procurement or development of a formal project management methodology to define and integrate the process, techniques and tools to be used, as well as the roles and responsibilities of the project stakeholders, team, project managers and line managers. General purpose methodologies such as PRINCE2 (OGC 2008), PROPS (Ericsson 1999) or derivations thereof are typically introduced at this stage. This is the simplest form of the Education (*what can be done*).

2. *Management Demand: Steering Groups and Sponsors*
   Steering groups and/or sponsors are put in place to foster use of the new methods and to ensure new skills learned during project management training are put into practice. This is the simplest form of management demand (*what should be done*). The caveat is that to be effective the managers involved require a good understanding of modern project management. Unfortunately this is rarely the case. While working as an external project management consultant I found that few of these managers possessed consistent or current knowledge about project management. I also found that in the vast majority of cases pressures of other work meant these managers were either unable or unwilling to spend time updating their skills in this area. The result is that many steering groups and sponsors are not in a position to judge what constitutes good project management execution and demand it from their project managers. This has two negative effects:

   a) Project managers will tend to prioritize their work according to their own perceived importance and not necessarily the priorities of the steering group/sponsor. They may neglect those deliverables perceived as not being necessary for their own work (for example, forecasts, or performance reporting using Earned Value) but important for effective governance. This leads to management and steering of the project that is less than its optimum.
   b) Instead of being managed by the sponsor/steering group senior project managers will tend to manage them, thus reversing the intention of the project governance hierarchy. This extends the agency problem with possible adverse effects for the corporation.

It can be seen from the above that steering groups and sponsors constitute the most severe skills bottleneck when it comes to good project management delivery in the industry. Further details of the Steering Group and Sponsor tasks are given in the next chapter.

3. *What is Done: Review of Projects in Trouble*
   The simplest form of '*what is done*' is to carry out reviews of troubled projects.

   Projects may end up in trouble due either to:

   • Project managers have neither the skills nor the training to be effective;

   or because:

   • Project managers do not apply the skills and techniques they learned during training effectively to the actual work.

The need for training and methodology use often arises from reviews of troubled projects. Unfortunately training employees in project management does not automatically guarantee that the trained behaviour is put into practice.

Three types of review of varying degrees of formality should be distinguished here:

1. *Audit.* This most formal type of review is often carried out by certified auditors from external organizations. It is usually indicated when the project places high financial amounts at stake, such as very large projects or those with public interest (for example, infrastructure projects). In such cases the audit is planned as part of the project planning, implementation and control phase.
2. *Formal Review.* Less rigorous than the audit, formal review is the most common type of assessment. It is often carried out by senior project managers from the same company but not necessarily from the same organization within the company. Projects are selected for review mainly because of lower than planned performance. The review process focuses primarily on project management; technical review of project achievements and deliverables may, or may not, be done as well.
3. *Health Check.* The health check is the most informal type of project management review. It is often carried out by as simple a process as sending a questionnaire to the project managers. Success of this type of review depends on the honesty and professionalism of the project manager involved, as his or her answers to the questionnaire cannot be independently verified. Thus this review type is not very credible unless the project manager is well known and held in high esteem by the company.

A number of templates for reviews and health checks exist, such as those published in the *Gower Handbook of Project Management* (Turner 2007).

All three of these review types require relatively small investment, which allows for continuity and a common process in project execution.

Having established Step 1, organizations improve project management quality in terms of the classic *iron triangle* of time, budget and quality goals. The measurement of project success along these goals has been around since the 1960s and is accepted today only within the context of other performance measures for project management. More details can be found in (Judgev and Müller 2005).

Step 2
Many corporations will use Step 1 techniques. Corporations with a medium amount (approx. 40–70 per cent) of project-based work tend to progress to Step 2 techniques in addition to those of Step 1.

Step 2 is the level to which the majority of projectized organizations have progressed. It is associated with Flexible Economist and Versatile Artist paradigms for project management governance.

Enablers:

- Acknowledgement of project management as a role within the organization.
- Definition of a career path for project managers.

Constraints:

- Insufficient amount of project-based business to warrant the investment.
- Strong organizational emphasis of the Conformist governance paradigm (Figure 3.3).

The *Education*, *Management Demand* and *What is Done* measures appropriate to Step 2 (Figure 3.2) are examined below:

1. *Education: External certification of project managers*
   External certification ensures that the professionalism of project managers is assessed independently by an organization dedicated to doing this. Two main approaches for certification exist:

   - Certification of knowledge, as in PMI's PMP®[1] certification.
   - Certification of skills, as in IPMA's Level C certification.

---

1   PMP is a registered certification mark of the Project Management Institute, Inc.

Certifications are valid for periods of 3 to 5 years and candidates must pursue training in project management to maintain their certification. Beside acknowledgement of professionalism, certification also reduces the agency problem between project sponsor and project manager, as it contributes to the credibility of the project manager (Turner and Müller 2004a). Certification of project managers became popular in the 1990s and is increasingly used by companies as a prerequisite for employment as project manager. Certification addresses *Education* at Step 2 of the model (Figure 3.2)

2. *Management Demand: Project Management Offices* (PMOs)
   Tactical PMOs are used to improve project management execution within the organization. PMOs are chartered with very diverse sets of tasks. Their project management governance charter typically starts with identification and reviewing of projects in trouble. Subsequently they work with the respective project managers to improve project management delivery. In addition, PMOs may identify skills gaps and train or consult project managers in methodologies, techniques and tools. Some PMOs take on even stronger governance roles by developing or deciding on the methodologies to use and the training programs for the project manager community in their organization. Such PMOs typically implement the other two measures of Step 2 and also Step 3 measures, thus becoming the unit which extends the organization's project management capabilities to a higher level. These PMOs are staffed with the most senior project management resources in order to leverage the skills and experience of these experts across the whole of the corporation. Tactical PMOs remain close to the individual projects and often form part of productive delivery in geography or functionality based units.

   A variation of the PMO approach is the Project Office (PO) or Project Support Office (PSO), which is staffed with administrative personnel to offload project administrative work thus relieving core project members, including the project manager, from the need to spend time on these overhead activities. Such POs and PSOs ensure good quality administrative work, appropriate documentation, planning data and status updates and thereby contribute to higher productivity of technical and management personnel.

   The tasks and charters of PMOs, POs and PSOs vary widely and are often designed to address the very specific approaches of their particular organization when it comes to project management delivery.

   Although PSOs and POs are important and useful, it is the tactical PMOs that determine the best practices for the community of project managers within their organization. They define what management expects from project managers thus addressing the *management demand* at Step 2 in the above model (Figure 3.2).

3. *What is Done: Mentor Programs*
   At Step 2 mentor programs identify and influence *what is done* by project managers. These programs (much more extensive than simple coaching) address the approach and attitude project managers develop towards their work as well as communication and teamwork with their teams, sponsors/ steering groups and project stakeholders. A variety of techniques exist. These range from internal swapping of managers from one organizational unit to another for a few hours each month, junior project managers being mentored by senior project managers or PMO members through to mentoring by external project management consultants. The aims are to improve co-operation between the project managers and other parts of the organization and to improve leadership skills for better project management delivery.

The best way to achieve a successful and economic implementation of Step 2 techniques is to ensure a healthy balance between the three Step 2 measures described above.

The assumption underlying implementation of this step is that project success is more complex than just the iron triangle. Step 2 techniques address a diverse set of Critical Success Factors (CSF) for projects and their surrounding organization, including:

- customer satisfaction
- appropriateness of planning techniques
- the general quality of project management
- the impact of project management on follow-on projects with customers.

Step 2 investments in project management improvement are generally higher than in Step 1 and so are the expected returns. Improvements are mainly at the project level and there is confidence that introduction of a PMO will have a beneficial impact on processes and practices of organizational units working in and around projects (Liu and Yetton 2007).

Step 3
The third step comprises introduction of advanced project management capabilities and is typically used by companies whose business consists almost entirely of project-based work. The underlying governance paradigm is Flexible Economist or Versatile Artist.

Enablers:

- management belief that competitors can only be bypassed through leapfrog, not gradual, improvements in capabilities
- belief that project management capabilities are a core corporate strength and constitute a major competitive advantage in the battle against others in the marketplace.

Constraints:

- lack of trust in the current project management resources' capabilities
- resistance to change corporate processes, roles and working-style to make them more supportive of project work
- unwillingness to prioritize project-based work over traditional hierarchies in the company.

Step 1 and Step 2 techniques are prerequisites (and always in active use) for these Step 3 techniques consisting of the following *Education, Management Demand* and *What is Done* measures examined below:

1. *Education: Advanced Training and Internal Certification*
   The Step 3 *Education* element consists of advanced training in particular areas requiring improvement, such as specialized planning tools, industry knowledge, technical skills, or other focused improvements of project management capabilities. Many companies at this step develop an internal certification program in which project managers are required to demonstrate the specific industry and technology skills peculiar to their own company's needs. They also need to prove their ability to run projects successfully using established project management principles. The amalgamation of management, technical and industry skills should allow for thought-leadership of project managers when working with the company's customers. These techniques move the *Education* to that of Step 3.

2. *Management Demand: Benchmarking*
   The Step 3 extension of *Management Demand* consists of benchmarking project management capabilities against those of other companies. Companies are benchmarked either against their competitors or across industries.

   Benchmarking against competitors is undertaken within industry clusters; companies of the same industry are assessed against a series of measurement dimensions and provided with assessment results showing their relative position against their competitors for each measurement dimension. This allows for identification of strengths and weaknesses relative to other companies in the same industry.

Benchmarking across industries allows for leapfrog improvements and development of enhanced capabilities, beyond those typical of the corporation's own industry. An example is benchmarking of relatively immature industries (in terms of project management) against the capabilities of more mature industries. This can result in rapid transfer of know-how. A good case in point is the way in which the IT industry, traditionally very weak in contract management, can learn from the contract management experts in the construction industry.

3. *What is Done: Maturity Model*
   Use of (organizational) project management maturity models addresses the Step 3 element *what is done*. These maturity models aim to ensure predictable and consistent delivery of good project results. Typically, they distinguish five levels of maturity ranging from ad-hoc to optimized, following the CMM model (SEI 1993). Most of these models assess project management capabilities only and provide one level of overall project management maturity. In contrast PMI's Organizational Project Management Maturity Model (OPM3) (PMI 2003) assesses project, program and portfolio management simultaneously and benchmarks the assessment results against a build-in database of best-practices for a number of industries. It then provides suggestions for improvement together with maturity levels measured across various dimensions. This allows for development of the organization's internal capabilities to manage their projects, resources and processes simultaneously and with maximum efficiency. Intuitively, these maturity models are also suitable for organizations at Step 1 and Step 2. However, the breadth and depth of the maturity model assessment questions, together with the sophistication of deployment of project, program and portfolio management related roles and skills require a strong organizational focus on project work, typical only of organizations at Step 3 and not to be expected of organizations at Step 1 and 2.

Once again, a healthy balance between the three Step 3 measures is required for their successful and economic implementation. No matter how far an organization develops, the techniques associated with the earlier Steps will not disappear. Step 3 organizations still apply Step 1 and Step 2 measures.

Step 3 requires the corporation to make significant investments, not just in terms of money but also in adapting and streamlining the organization's processes to make them more supportive of the project way of working and supportive only to a lesser extent of the traditional hierarchy.

Figure 3.3 summarizes the model by showing the incremental steps together with the enablers and constraints when moving from one step to the next. From left to right the organizational enablers develop from a project focus to project manager role and finally project management as a strategic capability of the corporation. Constraints arise from a narrow organizational focus on the technology development processes and their control at the expense of business and economic results. This focus usually results in a resistance to change for existing processes and practices because of the powerful position of technology heroes in the organization.

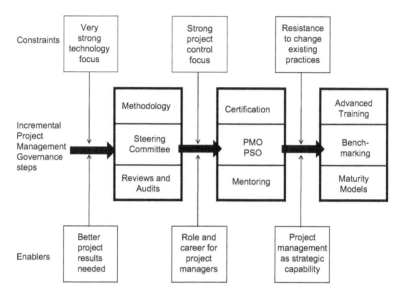

Figure 3.3   Model for governance of project management

Secondary elements of the framework

By taking program and portfolio management into account, we see that the measures for Steps 1–3 are also applicable in a wider context. Programs are groups of projects with a common goal, not achievable through just one project (Turner and Müller 2003). However, the steps and their contents are equally applicable for the governance of program management as they are for governance of project management. Examples are Program Management Offices, PMI's recently announced Program Manager Certification, PgMP[SM2] and its OPM3® maturity model.[3]

Portfolio management is the grouping of projects by their skills and resource needs. Governance of portfolio management is not developed to the same extent

---

2   PgMP is a service mark of the Project Management Institute, Inc.
3   OPM3 is a registered trade mark of the Project Management Institute, Inc.

as project and program management governance. Current practices comprise Step 1 measures, advanced training and PMI's OPM3® maturity model. It seems likely that the missing Step 2 measures will be developed in the near future.

ORGANIZATIONAL CONTEXT

The model in Figure 3.3 shows the importance of the organizational context for governance of project management. In a culture that fosters technological heroism over business results it is difficult to implement more advanced governance structures. This is caused by an underlying governance paradigm of Conformism and Agile Pragmatism established by successful and superior technologists in the days when projects were few and narrowly defined and with little resource sharing across projects. When companies develop towards more parallel and cross-sectional projects the need arises for a paradigm shift towards the Flexible Economist or Versatile Artist paradigm. This shift should be implemented using a management of change approach, taking into account such elements as:

- People and their behaviour.
- Goals and hidden agendas.
- What's in it for me?
- Willingness and ability to change.

Managing this paradigm shift requires a roadmap or framework as above and an organizational change process.

HOW MUCH PROJECT MANAGEMENT IS ENOUGH?

A word of caution: the governance model described above should not be misinterpreted. It does not imply that all organizations should aim for the highest step (that is, Step 3). It is not the same as a CMM model.

It is intended to identify the best economic mix of project management governance measures for an organization, with a healthy balance between the need for improving project management against increased investment. I have provided indicators on the correlation between the amount of project-based work in an organization and the appropriate step of the model to which you should aspire.

However, this cannot be generalized and careful evaluation is needed for each individual organization. The correct application of the model lies in the identification of the extent of project management needed (that is, which step is appropriate) and subsequently the balanced application of the measures given in that step of the model. The enablers show what needs to be in place from an organizational perspective to move up to a particular step. The constraints indicate threats to successful implementation. If too many constraints exist they should either be eliminated before moving to a particular step, or, if this is not possible, the move should be reconsidered. As every organization is different, there is no one size fits all solution. Many companies remain at Step 1 with no intention to move beyond it, while others aim for Step 2, starting with a PMO and project manager certification. Only a few companies aim for Step 3, as this requires a strong commitment to the project way of working as the mainstay of corporate culture.

KEY ROLES AND INDIVIDUALS IN THE FRAMEWORK

Implementing any or all of the nine measures (three at each step) in the framework requires two key roles, which should be carefully staffed. These are:

1. the sponsor, as representative of the steering group and closest to the project and its governance;
2. the PMO members, who work closely with the individual project managers on the application of appropriate methods and skills.

These two key roles are described in the subsections to follow.

The Sponsor

Researchers of project management agree on the important and often crucial role of project sponsors for project success (for example, Helm and Remington 2005, Müller and Turner 2002). In their research on effective project sponsorship Helm and Remington (2005, p. 57) found the following attributes of sponsors to be important:

- Appropriate seniority and power within the organization.
- Political knowledge of the organization and political savvy.
- Ability and willingness to make connections between project and organization.
- Courage and willingness to battle with others in the organization on behalf of the project.
- Ability to motivate the team to deliver the vision and provide ad hoc support to the project team.
- Willingness to partner with the project manager and project team.
- Excellent communication skills.
- Personal compatibility with other key players.
- Ability and willingness to provide objectivity and challenge the project manager.

Research carried out by Rodney Turner and me on the communication between sponsors and project managers, showed a significant difference in project performance, depending on the sponsor's interest in the project and willingness to communicate. When the sponsor showed more interest in the project together with a sceptical stance towards its performance they were rewarded with better project results (Müller and Turner 2002, Turner and Müller 2004).

The sponsor should therefore be experienced, socially competent and flexible in order to foster collaboration. At the same time he or she should be interested in project progress but sceptical and constantly challenging the project manager's interpretation of success. The sponsor should demand good project management work.

PMO members

Successful PMOs grow organically. Initially, they are setup with a senior expert in project management in order to establish PMO work in the organization and overcome resistance to the change inherent in building up new organizational entities. Especially important is the access to projects-in-trouble in order to help with their recovery. PMOs must build trust and gain credibility with individual project managers as well as provide visible examples of success to senior managers. They need to provide value up and down the organization. As the PMO grows more members with differing profiles are added to it.

Randy Englund and I used the metaphor of an organizational jungle to describe the personalities needed for successful PMO work. We suggest a three step evolution of PMO members (Englund and Müller 2005):

1. In the beginning there should be a *brown bear*. These animals are intelligent, have excellent navigation and long term memory. Bear people in organizations have a deep introspective capacity, are caring, compassionate, seekers of deeper self-knowledge, dreamers at times and helpers. They have tremendous power and physical strength, intelligence, inner confidence, reserve and detachment. They draw great strength from solitude, choose peace instead of conflict and contemplate the healing power. Their contribution is strength, introspection and self-knowledge.

    Managers establishing a PMO should be of this profile. By building on long years of experience and their patience and the credibility gained within the organization, they build collaborative relationships with the individual project managers and work with them on the improvement of their skills and project results. They build a reputation of the PMO as a trusted partner and a source for valuable information and support. PMOs at this stage are often staffed with one or two individuals. With a successful launch of the

PMO, the capacity of this group is quickly reached and further resources are needed. These additional people, however, need to be of a different profile.

2. PMOs in growth mode need *lions*. Lions roar in concert to scare away their enemies. In PMO context this means lions are needed to communicate the PMO messages, including best-practices in managing the organization's projects and the benefits of certification etc. These PMO members are typically mid-career project managers with a few years of experience. They are temporarily assigned to the PMO, maybe for 2–3 years, to act as a role model for the more junior project managers and to foster good project management work in the organization. Then they move on to other responsibilities. These tactical PMOs, concerned with governance of project management at the operational level, can exist for an extended period of time. However, over time they need a strategic vision, which does not grow organically among their peers.

3. In the long term PMOs need *eagles*. These animals hover at high altitudes; constantly monitoring what is happening at ground level and can be on the ground within seconds. In an organizational context these people see the broader strategic picture of project, program and portfolio governance, often far beyond the boundaries of the own organization. At the same time, they can work 'top down' through to the detail level. They work, for example, on the details of a portfolio management tool to identify the best tool for the organization, or do reviews at the project level to identify skill shortages. These individuals are hard to find as they combine both breadth and depth in their approach to work. Their contribution is, however, key for the long term survival of the PMO.

The metaphor used above shows the migration of personalities within a PMO. The three sets of personal attributes are not mutually exclusive. In fact, stronger PMO organizations carefully employ members to ensure a good balance between the three profiles.

This chapter has shown a framework for governance of the project management capabilities of individuals, organizations and entire firms or corporations. The next chapter addresses governance of portfolios and programs within organizations.

CHAPTER 4

GOVERNANCE OF PROGRAMS AND PORTFOLIOS

This chapter introduces the governance of programs and portfolios. It opens with a company-wide perspective and discusses the relationship between corporate success and choice of governance approach for programs and portfolios. It then presents the particular governance function of both.

PROGRAMS AND PORTFOLIOS AS A FORM OF GOVERNANCE

The board of directors makes fundamental decisions on how the business of a corporation will be conducted. In the vast majority of organizations part of corporate business will be performed through repetitive operations, for example, manufacturing. The other part will be conducted through projects, that is, the one-off upgrades of manufacturing capabilities, new product development and customer delivery projects. At any one point in time the project part of the corporation consists of a larger or smaller number of ongoing projects being run simultaneously. As these projects typically compete for a finite number of often scarce resources, they need to be governed. The focus is on:

- Ensuring *effectiveness* by 'doing the right projects'.
- Ensuring *efficiency* by 'doing projects right'.

Effectiveness is achieved through selection and prioritization of those projects that contribute most to corporate strategy. They create the highest value for the corporation and therefore constitute the most economic use of scarce resources. This need for effectiveness has led to the development of the project portfolio approach. The project portfolio is a grouping of projects and programs by similar skills or resource needs, prioritized by their contribution to corporate strategy and managed together to optimize contribution to strategic objectives. Thus, project portfolio management is concerned with managing competing needs for scarce skills and competing needs for scarce resources, of the various projects in the portfolio.

Efficiency can be improved through effective use of programs. Programs are groupings of projects by common objective unable to be realized with a single project alone. Efficiency is achieved through minimizing costs of converting *input* to *output* within and across projects with a common goal, that is, a program. These costs are known as transaction costs within TCE (Transaction Costs Economics).

A TCE (Williamson 1985) perspective (as described in Chapter 1) shows that programs and portfolios achieve balance between effectiveness and efficiency by:

a) Providing a product 'fit for purpose' that is done through program management This implies the constant adaptation of project outcomes to changing market needs.
b) Lowering of overall costs by economizing existing scales and resources that is done through portfolio management.

The board of directors makes the decision on whether and how to use programs and portfolios as an approach to implementing the project-based part of the organization. This decision determines the framework for managers to decide on the types of project in which the organization is going to engage. In this way, the management board decision sets the governance framework.

Through our global research (Blomquist and Müller 2006) we found that the project based part of the organization is typically governed by management decisions on:

• whether, when and how to share resources across projects;
• whether to pursue higher level goals which need to be accomplished through a number of interlinked projects;
• or whether to focus on smaller goals, which can be accomplished by individual projects.

This leads to four possible governance structures for project based organizations, as shown in Figure 4.1.

As illustrated, organizations choose between:

• Maximizing the return on individual and independent projects in a *multi-project organization*. Such organizations implement independent projects with objectives that are not related to each other. Nor do they aim at resource sharing across projects. Projects in this type of organization are very diverse and have little or nothing in common, thus there are no synergies of objectives or resource usage. In a *multi-project organization* the underlying business strategy is matching particular skill sets of the individuals within the organization to project needs, or using external resources with very specific skill sets for just the duration of a contracted project.
• Maximizing the effectiveness by using existing skill sets and contributions to strategic objectives through a *portfolio of projects*. Such organizations

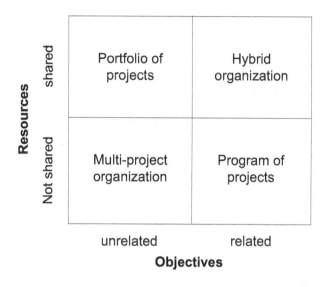

Figure 4.1   Four different governance styles

group their projects based on availability of skill sets and prioritize their projects to maximize their strategic objectives. The objectives of projects in a portfolio do not necessarily have to be related to each other; key is commonality of skill sets required.

• Maximizing the efficiency by using *programs of projects*. Such organizations emphasize synergies stemming from combining several individual project objectives into a larger overall objective. In this case it is imperative that the individual projects within the program share common objectives. Skill sets needed may vary significantly between the individual programs.

• Balancing maximization of effectiveness and efficiency through a combination of program and portfolio approaches into a *hybrid organization*. Such organizations achieve their strategic objectives by combining sharing of skill sets through portfolios and relating project objectives through programs.

As can be seen from Figure 4.2, corporate performance varies greatly according to the choice of governance approach. Corporations that use the hybrid approach of combining and balancing program and portfolio management are statistically significantly more successful than corporations using any one of the other three approaches. Corporations that use the multi-project approach achieve the lowest level of performance, while corporations that predominantly use either the program *or* portfolio management approach achieve better performance than multi-project corporations but worse performance than hybrid ones. Although the program and portfolio management approach is shown, in Figure 4.2, to achieve marginally better performance than the multi-project approach the difference is not statistically significant. Performance in this case is measured as the sum of performances at project, program and portfolio level. The measurement scale on the left hand side indicates the average level of performance on a scale from zero to one. Hybrid organizations achieved 70 per cent of the possible maximum of performance, whereas program or portfolio driven organizations achieved approximately 50 per cent of their potential performance. Multi-project organizations achieved about a third of the maximum possible performance.

The research summarized by Figure 4.2, supports the importance of simultaneous program and portfolio management for good corporate results. The hybrid approach balances both efficiency and effectiveness when deciding which projects to take on and which ones to drop. It has been empirically shown to deliver the best results.

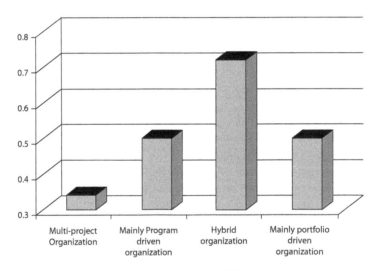

Figure 4.2   Organizational performance in different governance structures

GOVERNANCE OF PROJECT PORTFOLIOS

The objective of project portfolio governance is to ensure that the best projects are selected; that is, those that will achieve their strategic objectives in the shortest possible time, within the constraints of available skills and resources. The projects and programs in any given portfolio are screened, selected, prioritized and scheduled based on getting the highest possible throughput of the 'best' projects[1]

---

1   The term 'project' is used synonymous with 'projects and programs' throughout the rest of this section.

for the organization (Kendall and Rollins 2003). In this context the term *throughput*, used by Kendall and Rollins in their book on strategic portfolio management and the PMO, implies ensuring the greatest number of the *best* projects implemented by the organization in the shortest possible amount of time. The term *best* is also defined as a combination of good quality and optimum throughput; that is, a large number of *good* projects might be preferable to a much smaller number of *excellent* projects as the overall throughput will be greater.

A prerequisite of effective portfolio management is an appropriate communication structure that allows information flow from portfolios to projects and back again. Portfolio managers often communicate portfolio decisions to line or middle management, sponsors (and steering groups). Tactical PMOs collect and aggregate project performance to the portfolio level. This is shown in Figure 4.3. Tactical PMOs are close to projects at the operational level. This, together with a portfolio management tool for capturing project level performance data, allows aggregation of this data to the portfolio level for portfolio level decision making. In addition, aggregated performance data are provided not only to portfolio management, but also to line management, such as Steering Groups and resource pool managers. This information flow is shown by solid lines in Figure 4.3, below.

Almost as a by-product effective aggregated project performance data provides for portfolio reporting, identification of project resource needs, identification of project management weaknesses and associated areas that are candidates for project manager training. Control-oriented PMOs often own the project manager training curriculum and either provide training themselves or coordinate training for the community of project managers.

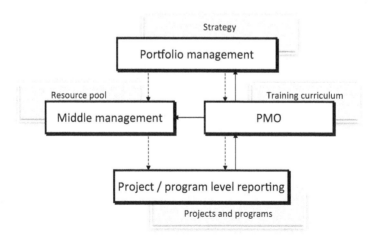

Figure 4.3   Information and action flow linking strategy and projects

In Figure 4.3 above, resulting actions are shown by dotted lines. As a result of reported performance, portfolio management may initiate actions down the hierarchy either via the middle management route (for example, for provision of required resources for a project) or the PMO route (for example, for improvement of project management capabilities). This information and action flow links the strategy level of the organization (represented by portfolio management) with the project level of the organization (represented by project managers) through aggregation and filtering at the PMO and middle management levels. The quality of this information flow determines the strength of the linkage between strategy and projects, hence the organization's capability to implement strategy effectively through projects.

An important purpose of project portfolio governance is to provide the objectives for each portfolio, which should be derived from the organization's strategy. These objectives provide the framework for decision making within the portfolio. They vary depending upon whether the corporation is shareholder- or stakeholder-oriented. Ensuring objectives are achieved involves careful selection and prioritization of the projects within each portfolio to ensure alignment with its own individual portfolio objectives.

Through their research Cooper, Edgett and Kleinschmidt (2004a, 2004b, 2004c) identified the three most often used portfolio optimization strategies, which are either used alone or in combination with each other. These are:

1. *Value Maximization.* Projects are selected for the portfolio if they reach a certain threshold value. This is often a financial measure such as Return on Investment (ROI) or Net Present Value (NPV). The strategy is often criticized as being too numbers focused and for not factoring in the more qualitative benefits of each project. Research has shown that corporations who use this as a standalone strategy perform worst in their industry.
2. *Balancing.* This strategy works in a similar way to an investment fund. Projects are selected into the portfolio based on a balanced weighted measure of a number of parameters. Examples are:
   – distribution of high versus low risk projects
   – distribution of short term versus long term projects.
   The balancing algorithm uses a number of two-dimensional graphs for each parameter to visualize the relative positions of projects against each other, allowing managers to select the most desirable balance of projects. The strategy is criticized for lack of guidance on the balancing parameters and weighting criteria. Research has shown that corporations who use this as a standalone strategy are more successful in their industry than those who use Value Maximization as a standalone strategy.

3. *Strategic Alignment*. This strategy assigns a budget value to each strategic objective of the corporation. It is also called the *strategic bucket* approach. When a project is considered for the portfolio it is tested against the objectives of each bucket (that is, the strategic goal). If the project supports one of the goals, then it is funded out of the relevant bucket. This strategy requires detailed planning, based on a long term view anticipating future business trends. Therefore it is often criticized for being too hypothetical. Research has shown, however, that corporations who use this as a standalone strategy are the most successful in their industry.

The three strategies described above are akin to shareholder theory (*Value Maximization*) and stakeholder theory (*Balancing*). *Strategic Alignment* potentially supports both shareholder and stakeholder theories, as it is contingent on the corporation's strategy.

Governance of project portfolios also includes provision of the means to achieve portfolio objectives. This includes roles, authorities and decisions on the degree to which the portfolio management process is formalized.

Roles and authorities assigned from the governance institution to the portfolio managers include:

- Business management roles and authorities:
  - Participation in corporate business planning.
  - Special emphasis on contributing to planning for changes in required skill sets and resources.
  - Procurement of the agreed-upon quantity and quality of skill sets.
- Portfolio decision roles and authorities:
  - Determination of roles.
  - Identification of individuals with the authority to identify, prioritize and select projects within portfolios.
  - Includes responsibility and authority to start, suspend or terminate projects from within a portfolio.
- Portfolio maintenance roles and authorities:
  - Collection and aggregation of reports.
  - Participation in steering groups and project/program plan reviews.
  - Identification of bad projects and associated initiation of reviews, handling of issues and so on.
  - Coaching of project managers.
  - General improvement of organizational processes.

The degree to which the portfolio management process is formalized, is influenced by the complexity of the decision making process in the organization. The more factors that need to be taken into account for a portfolio decision (that is, the more complex the organization is), the more formalized portfolio management becomes. Structured and formal portfolio management is supported by:

- Computer-based portfolio management applications, which automate status calculations, forecasts, scenario analysis and other numerical analysis. The output of these applications provides input to the decisions portfolio managers make.
- Structured reporting of all projects in each portfolio, using similar metrics for all projects. This allows *like for like* comparisons of project results and forecasts, supporting better, more informed, decision making.
- Open communication of project priorities and results. This is done by using company-wide standard tools for collecting and disseminating information about all projects in the portfolio and by using similar metrics for all project reports. This not only supports open communication but also provides for general transparency within the corporation, a major objective of corporate governance policies and laws (for example, SOX and others).

The third major governance function, control of portfolio performance to attain stated portfolio objectives, is achieved through performance control and enabling of knowledge management.

Research on high performing companies has shown that portfolio performance can be measured by using three groups of performance variables (Müller, Martinsuo and Blomquist 2008):

1. *Achievement of desired portfolio results.* These are aggregated project level measures. They are similar to the most common measures of corporate success (not just project success). The measures of customer satisfaction, achieved time, cost, quality results and user requirements are determined for each project, along with the financial results of the portfolio itself. The individual project measures are then evaluated and conclusions are drawn for portfolio adjustments. These measures are strongly impacted by the reporting structure within the organization. Higher performing organizations use steering groups for project governance, organization-wide tools to collect and disseminate project status information and implement project progress reporting using organization-wide standard measures.
2. *Achievement of project/program purpose.* These are summary level measures. They show how well the projects and programs in the portfolio have fulfilled their purpose. Organizations scoring high on this measure are committed to always making decisions in the best overall interests of the organization, selecting projects in accordance with corporate strategy, prioritizing their projects and communicating these priorities across the organization.

3. *Balancing priorities*. These are business level measures. They measure achievement of the broader interests by using a balancing algorithm for a number of individual business measures. These include resource retention, timely implementation of programs and stakeholder satisfaction. Balance is achieved by project, program and portfolio managers keeping a broader view of the business priorities. They do not compromise portfolio results for the success of a single project. This is in stark contrast to traditional project management practices. Traditionally, project managers are remunerated for delivering their individual projects in accordance with the original plan (on time, within budget and with just the planned resources). The project managers insist on resource availability with just their own individual project's interests in mind, no matter what harm that might cause to the general good of the company itself. Awareness has grown in recent years that project managers, just as program and portfolio managers, should be compensated based on their overall contribution to corporate objectives and not just the perceived individual success of the projects they manage. (Turner and Müller 2003).

The above three groups of measures for portfolio performance should be assessed at each portfolio reporting cycle. Possible deviations will need to be corrected using the underlying variables described above.

A further factor for portfolio performance involves enabling knowledge management at the portfolio level itself. This may sound contrary to common wisdom, which dictates that knowledge management is done at the project level. However, the various forms of knowledge management can be enabled at the portfolio level by individual portfolio managers insisting on (and often funding) knowledge capturing in projects. This is in line with the benefits of knowledge management accruing at the portfolio level.

Knowledge management in this context is far more than collecting, saving and disseminating documents and experiences from individual projects. Knowledge management is also about the deliberate investment in learning projects. Payback for this investment is greater efficiency and higher customer satisfaction in the long term (Andersson and Müller 2007).

I did some research on knowledge management together with Annika Andersson (Andersson and Müller 2007). The results showed that organizations that aim for long-term relationships with their customers and starting from the very first projects, deliberately invest in learning about their customers' business and processes, achieve better long-term project results. The research found that portfolio level business results achieved over time through this type of strategic thinking are better than those stemming from a 'learn just as much as needed'/ 'need to know' approach to delivering projects to the customer. In addition to good financial and customer satisfaction results, this strategic approach also fosters a long term business relationship that yields continuously ongoing projects. This is known as the *first mover advantage* in TCE.

Last, but not least, the question of choosing appropriate portfolio managers needs to be addressed by the governance institution for portfolios. What is an appropriate level of authority and position in the corporate hierarchy? Research has shown that portfolio management is normally carried out as a team activity. Teams consist primarily of higher level managers in the portfolio's particular area of specialization, such as a team of R&D managers, headed by a Vice President of the corporation. Some companies may additionally employ specialists for portfolio evaluation and risk management in order to balance larger portfolios for a constant flow of new products at the lowest possible risk. This allows complex evaluations of inter-project relationships and associated risks in a portfolio, together with complex scenario analyses and forecasts. The managers that have decision authority at the portfolio level are most often company executives with positions like Vice President, Managing Director, Business Unit Manager or Country Manager etc. Remuneration of these executives is aligned with corporate objectives and their performance reported through the company's annual report. They are the managers accountable for implementing corporate strategy (Blomquist and Müller 2006). Therefore executives at this level are the ones most qualified to lead the portfolio management teams.

Summarizing what we have said about the governance of project portfolios in this section:

- We see corporate strategy as the main driver for setting portfolio objectives.
- Project portfolio governance supports these corporate objectives by:
  - Identification of the portfolio management team and its head to ensure the appropriate decision level for the organization.
  - Agreeing on the optimization strategy for project portfolios.
  - Deciding on the depth and formalization of portfolio roles and processes with the portfolio managers.

Progress reporting and control is done by assessing and balancing how well portfolio, customer and wider organizational objectives have been achieved. This performance feedback may be used to adjust and refine corporate strategy for the upcoming reporting periods.

GOVERNANCE OF PROGRAMS

The aim of governance of programs is to ensure achievement of a major objective or benefit, which cannot be achieved by a single project alone, as efficiently as possible. This is achieved through the sum of outputs and synergies of a number of individual projects; the projects that comprise the program. The main areas of concern at the program level are the management of benefits and stakeholders, as well as governance of the projects within the program (PMI 2006b).

We now take a close look at exactly what we mean by *a program (of projects)*.

It would be a mistake to think of a program as 'simply a large project broken up into easily manageable parts'. Programs are not simply large projects. Projects deliver a measurable, often physical output, whereas programs often deliver benefits that are less tangible, at least in the early stages.

A good example of a program is the NASA Apollo program in the 1960s which had, as its major objective, establishing a reputation for NASA as the leading space exploration agency. Each Apollo mission was a project within the program (including sending men to the moon), but the major objective could only be achieved by the sum of the results of all the individual projects. Initially, the achievement associated with this major objective was intangible (reputation); later it became more tangible in form of industry contracts and funding.

A further example is the Öresund link, which connects eastern Denmark (that is, Copenhagen) with southern Sweden (that is, Malmö). The link consists of a tunnel leading from Denmark to an artificial island in the Öresund (the body of water between Denmark and Sweden) and then a bridge to Sweden. Impressive as this construction is, with its tunnel, island and bridge, it is not a program but a single project which is part of a larger program. The program has as its major objective the economic growth of the entire Öresund region. The Öresund link enables easy communication and flow of people and goods across the borders of Denmark and Sweden. However, it requires many more projects to establish economic growth. This includes agreement on employment and taxation issues for commuters (defined in the context of the program as people working in one country but living in the other), harmonization of communication and other infrastructure including telephone fees and public services. The success of the program is less tangible as it is measured by an increase in investor perception of the region as being supportive of their business needs.

Let us look at the types of programs that exist.

Two main forms of program exist, each with its own major implication for program governance. These are:

1. *Temporary Programs*. This type of program has a defined end date. As with a project this program is a temporary organization aiming to achieve a defined benefit by a specific date.

   An example is implementing a new Enterprise Resource Planning (ERP) system, such as SAP or others, by incremental rollouts over time. The program is made up of a number of projects over an extended period of time, constituting a roadmap of business functions to be supported at each rollout through new or enhanced IT facilities. The success of the program as a whole will be measured once the final rollout has been successfully implemented and the program is finished. The program's objective setting, planning, budgeting and scheduling is, at least to a large extent, done during the early stages of the program.

   This type of program is often governed primarily with control in mind; that is, control of milestone achievements, use of Stage Gate Reviews and use of mitigation strategies to reduce risks constraining achievement of the plan.

2. *Semi-permanent Programs*. This type of program has no defined end date. It remains active, for example, as long as there is a market for the product or service it produces. These programs include not only projects, but also operational processes. The program is terminated only by a specific event, such as when the product being produced is decommissioned.

   An example is a new model of a car. The new model will be manufactured continuously and receive its annual face-lift (in form of projects) as long as there is a market for that model. The end date of such a program is not foreseeable at the time of program launch; the program will only end when the model is no longer viable in the marketplace and is superseded and decommissioned.

   The objectives for this type of program are often visionary and can only be vaguely estimated at the start. Program planning and budgeting is often done on an annual basis, which means that next year's budget is unknown as is the extent to which the program can expand or must contract. These programs require a more entrepreneurial approach to governance than the temporary programs. Change is continuously encouraged, for example, to make the car model more attractive for the market. Achievements and forecasts are evaluated in certain intervals and program plans adapted to changing circumstances.

PMI (2006b) defines program governance as the process for developing, communicating, implementing, monitoring and assuring the policies, procedures, organizational structures and practices for a program. It provides a framework for decision making and is guided by strategic management, portfolio management and any cross-program governance directives. Governance is executed by the Executive Sponsor and their Program Steering Committee. These committees consist of a Business Change Manager, Portfolio Manager and other stakeholders (as needed), plus the Executive Sponsor of the program. The Program Manager reports to the Steering Committee.

The aim of program governance is to be an enabler for the aspired program benefits by setting a framework allowing for a coordinated and efficient execution of the program and the projects of which it consists.

Goal Setting

The purpose of the governance function of *goal setting* is to ensure that the proposed program is feasible and its required prerequisites are either already in place or will be when needed. It must ensure that the proposed program, its methods (processes, tools and techniques), facilities, skill sets and the context it creates (for example, the specialist to be employed, market segments to be targeted and so on). fit into the culture and objectives of the overall corporation and its existing policies. On occasion, however, a program may be of such high importance that it needs to be run outside of the day-to-day project work of the corporation. Typically, such programs aim for major change, renewal or repositioning of the corporation as a whole or revamping its entire product set.

Effective *goal setting* needs to address:

- Identification and communication of the program's *contribution to the portfolio objectives* of the corporation. This includes the program's qualitative and quantitative performance measures (including tolerance levels), together with their emergence over time.
- Defining the goals and establishing agreement on the 'three themes' of program management as established by PMI (2006b):

    1. *Benefits management*
       Benefits management consists of defining the program's benefits and agreement on a plan for how best to manage attaining them. The program's governance institution (typically a Program Steering Committee) identifies the benefits. The benefits management plan itself is developed by program management and outlines the benefits of the program within the known constraints (for example, financial and time budgets, risks and so on). The nature of the benefits management plan is likely to differ, depending on the type of program being implemented.

    – *Temporary programs*

The benefits management plan for temporary programs is at a detailed level for near term planning but at an order of magnitude level for medium to long term planning, especially when the program's long term benefits are beyond the organization's planning cycle.

    – *Semi-permanent programs*

The benefits management plan for semi-permanent programs is at a detailed level for the immediate future, but at a higher, possibly even visionary level, for long term benefits.

The benefits management plan serves as input to program planning and becomes a major tool for progress control during program implementation.

2. *Stakeholder management*

Stakeholder management consists of defining the objectives for how to manage the different stakeholder groups. This includes determining that certain stakeholders have priority over others and the intended level of involvement of such stakeholders.

3. *Project governance*

Project governance consists of identifying any possible constraints for governance of the projects comprising the program, for example, legal constraints on using specific project management methodologies and so on.

• General Program Governance Practices. This includes definition of the program's success criteria, contracting and contract management practices, depth and accuracy of planning and control within the program, reporting and communication standards, as well as procedures for escalation, risk handling, resource procurement and safety.

Achievement of Program Objectives

According to research, the means of achieving program objectives are the budgets, skills and other resources needed (Blomquist and Müller 2006). This research also established a need for appropriate:

• *Organization structures* include relevant program hierarchy which allows for decision making at the appropriate level, so that flexibility in program execution is balanced with the need for central and formal decision making. Programs need to be flexible and respond quickly to changing circumstances, which means that resources in the program need to be able to be re-assigned and projects suspended, stopped or cancelled on short notice if necessary.

An effective organizational structure will balance the ability to change quickly against the need for appropriate management control.

* *Roles and authorities* to be assigned by the program steering committee. In addition to the program management role these include:
    - *Opportunity management roles and authorities*: Identification of new business opportunities as well as any synergies that may exist between currently ongoing projects and programs. Resources in these roles need to be close to the organizations expected to receive the benefits of the program, thus allowing for effectiveness and efficiency in program execution.
    - *Resource management roles and authorities*: Planning ahead for the specific resource and skill set requirements of each program. The purpose is to facilitate ease of selection of appropriate candidates from the internal pool of resources or to establish a need for external resources, if necessary.
    - *Program maintenance roles and authorities*: Collection and aggregation of project and program status reports, participation in steering groups, Stage Gate Reviews, identification and review of poorly performing projects within the program, handling of issues in the program, coaching of project managers and general improvement of organizational processes.
* *Program Management Office support.* Ideally the steering group, as a governance institution, should decide to establish a dedicated Program Management Office. As described in Chapter 2, this can be either an expert team whose function is to support the choice of methods and application of tools and techniques, or an administrative team whose function is to relieve the productive program resources from the need to do unproductive administrative work, that is, a Program Support Office. The decision criteria for deciding which to use will include evaluating the gains to be achieved by the current program and contrasting them against the possibility of wider organizational synergies and longer term corporate wide enhancement of skill sets.
* *Choosing appropriate program managers.* Just as programs differ from projects, so does the role of program managers differ from that of project managers. While the project managers are more focused on strict planning, management and solving of technical issues, program managers are tolerant of uncertainty, embrace change and are more aware of wider business influences (Pellegrinelli et al. 2003). A study by Partington, Pellegrinelli and Young (2005) showed that program mangers, in contrast to project managers, must feel comfortable in a continuously changing and ambiguous work environment. They identify seventeen attributes of program managers at four levels. The seventeen attributes are grouped into those representing the relationship between program managers and:

  - the program work itself
  - the program team
  - the program environment

The four levels of program manager range from:

- *Level 1*: Concern that the scope of the program is effectively delivered. This lowest level of program manager is mainly concerned with detailed planning and reuse of procedural solutions that have worked well in the past.
- *Level 2:* Concern for the wider organizational impact of the program. These are managers in the traditional sense, detached, delegating, but still able to adapt to the specific circumstances of the program. They are concerned with effective execution of the program but also its impact on the surrounding organization.
- *Level 3*: Concern for the achievement of high-level program outcomes. These managers use their corporate social intelligence and their high commitment to success to overcome obstacles, motivate and exploit the talents of others and plan for contingencies. They are aware of the pace with which their environment can absorb change and adapt the program accordingly.
- *Level 4*: Concern for development of strategic capabilities. Just like the eagle described in Chapter 3, these managers can take on several roles, from detailed work to strategic thinking. They are inspirational, charismatic and culturally sensitive leaders, able to adapt the environment to suit their purposes. They are very future oriented and can portray the program within an external context.

The suitable profile of a program manager for any given program depends on the nature, size and complexity of the program. The four levels above indicate not only the managers' profile, but also particular attributes that may or may not be needed in a given program. These four levels also parallel, at least roughly, the four governance paradigms. Levels 1 and 2 relate to behaviour control, the Conformist and Agile Pragmatist paradigms respectively, whereas levels 3 and 4 parallel attributes found respectively in the Flexible Economist and Versatile Artist paradigms. Thus, looking for overlap between the organization's governance paradigm, program needs and program manager attributes helps in identifying suitable program managers.

Controlling progress

Controlling progress, the third governance function, is concerned with the measurement of contributions to the portfolio objectives, program level achievements in terms of benefits and general plan adherence. Just as projects are controlled at phase end, milestone or Stage Gate Reviews, so are programs. PMI

(2006b) suggests conducting a Stage Gate Review at the end of each program phase. These reviews compare plans and achievements, assess and evaluate performance, lessons learned and risks in order to decide on continuation, suspension or modification of the program.

The level and frequency of control will be synchronized with the governance needs of the program and the information needs of the steering committee. This is especially of concern for programs within larger organizations, where Stage Gate Reviews must be synchronized with the fundamental (mega-) processes of the corporation. Programs in their early stages are often only loosely coupled to the corporation's mega-processes (for example, the fundamental sales and marketing process). In these stages feasibility studies, technology research studies, marketing studies and others are performed in parallel. It is not until the second or third Milestone or Stage Gate Review (depending on the corporate methodology) that the results of the different studies are combined into an overall evaluation of the future of the program. The program steering group, as the governance institution, coordinates these activities, puts the required teams in place, controls progress and evaluates the results together with portfolio management for a go or no-go decision.

Once the program is accepted the steering committee reviews the program in accordance with the program management methodology. PMI (2006b) suggests, as a minimum, a Stage Gate Review at the end of each of the phases:

- Pre-program setup, where the principal feasibility of the program idea is reviewed and a decision on whether to invest in further planning and feasibility studies is made.
- Program setup, where the program management and benefits management plans are reviewed and decisions made on the level of investment required to establish the necessary infrastructure.
- Establishing the program and technical infrastructure, where the suitability of the infrastructure is reviewed and the decision on the level of investment in the projects for benefit creation is made.
- Benefits delivery, when the intended benefits have been created, or the market for the product no longer exists and a decision on closing the program is to be made.
- Closing the program, when the program is finished and subsequent benefits (for example, through maintenance of existing products) are handed over to the appropriate organization.

It is possible that a need for reviews between the above Stage Gate Reviews may emerge, especially in multi-year programs with extended benefits delivery phases. In these cases periodic reviews are needed to keep the program aligned with corporate strategy.

SUMMARY

Program governance shares some common ground with project governance. This includes:

- Deciding on a suitable governance approach depending on contract type.
- The principal-agent relationship between steering committee and project or program manager and associated communication structures.
- The fit of the governance structure to the organization's governance paradigm.

Specific aspects of the common ground between governance of programs and projects are covered in the next chapter.

Within this chapter I addressed program and portfolio management as a governance structure for project-based organizations and looked at the respective corporate performance of different governance structures. Then the specific goals, means and control mechanisms for governance of portfolios and programs were addressed. The next chapter describes the governance of projects.

CHAPTER 5

GOVERNANCE OF PROJECTS

This chapter introduces the role of the steering group as the main institution for governance of projects. It considers the different roles and tasks in the governance of the project as a transaction and as an agency then reviews the different contract types and their implications for governance of projects and addresses governance of the link between parent and project organization by looking at the combined effect of structure, contract, communication and risk. In the final part of the chapter I address the question of identifying appropriate project managers for the different types of project.

The aim of project governance is the consistent and predictable delivery of the project's planned contribution to the portfolio – and thereby to the achievement of the corporation's strategic objectives – within the framework of corporate governance. Therefore project governance is intimately linked with corporate governance. Project governance provides risk minimization, transparency, division of ownership and control at the project level.

Governance models or guidelines, such as those presented in Chapter 2, are developed from different perspectives. Research by Klakegg et al. (2008) on governance frameworks for large public projects showed that these frameworks are developed using either a *top-down* or a *bottom-up* approach. Top-down approaches are developed from an outcome perspective and represent the Flexible Economist and Versatile Artist paradigm, whereas bottom-up approaches take a control perspective and are developed as an extension of existing project management methodologies, such as PRINCE2. Bottom-up approaches represent the Conformist and Agile Pragmatist paradigm.

This distinction has implications for the depth to which governance is carried out by the institutions governing projects. A control perspective calls for more upfront planning and estimation, strict control procedures and contingency plans, whereas an outcome perspective provides more flexibility in project execution as long as the governance institution feels comfortable that the project's intended outcome can be achieved.

THE STEERING GROUP

The steering group is the principle institution for project governance. Although the steering group may not always be the only institution for governance of projects, it is the institution that carries the most authority when it comes to project execution. The steering group has ultimate responsibility for project success; therefore it owns the business case and is accountable to upper management for achievement of the intended project outcome, objectives and benefits.

Steering group members are decision-makers and it is essential that they have managerial authority to assign or withdraw resources (for example, financial) from the project. They also must have authority to accept or decline proposed changes to the project. They are the ultimate authority that rules on whether the project has accomplished its objectives or not.

Steering groups also constitute the linkage between the permanent and the temporary organization. By being a part of both organizations, one of their responsibilities is to ensure effective coordination of governance mechanisms between the project and its parent organization.

Research by Crawford et al. (2008) showed that sponsors and by association the steering group, look at the interface between the permanent and temporary organizations from two opposite perspectives:

1. *The perspective of the parent organization towards its project.* This includes defining the goals, means and ends of the project, its contribution to and link with the parent organization. This is project governance.
2. *The perspective of the project towards its parent organization.* This includes provision of resources, decisions, formal decisions like sign-off on milestones by the parent organization and, where appropriate, formal authorization by the parent organization for the project to continue. This is project support.

Depending on its individual specific situation, a project may have a higher or lower need for support and governance. Typically, high governance is indicated, for example (Crawford et al. 2008):

- in cases where project failure would lead to very severe consequences;
- when the project is mission critical;
- when the parent organization works in rapidly changing markets;
- where corporate governance requires a strong focus on a particular project;
- the project must be realigned to a new strategy.

Typically, high support is indicated for projects that:

- lack resources and other support from the parent organization;
- incur resistance from within the parent organization to accept the project or its outcome;
- have inexperienced project management.

Based on specific governance or support needs of a project, its steering group coordinates the link and synchronizes the efforts between the permanent and temporary organizations.

The governance tasks of the steering group include establishing the governance infrastructure, in addition to the previously discussed tasks of goal definition, provision of the means to achieve those goals and control of progress.

To carry out these tasks, the steering group assumes the roles outlined in the following section.

Roles of the steering group

Governance infrastructure
The steering group sets up *the governance infrastructure* by defining and communicating to all appropriate parts of the organization, upwards and downwards:

- the project governance processes;
- the means of controlling projects;
- the roles, responsibilities and approval authorities.

Also, this infrastructure framework will need to link easily into existing corporate governance and cross organizational procedures, corporate policies, existing standards and processes.

Depending upon its underlying governance paradigm, each organization will setup the governance infrastructure framework in different ways. Behaviour oriented paradigms (Conformist and Agile Pragmatist) will lead to a governance framework that is more process and control oriented, stressing the need for planning and plan conformance, a process discipline and clear lines of responsibility. Outcome oriented paradigms (Flexible Economist and Versatile Artist) will lead to a governance framework that gives more trust and autonomy to the project itself and focus more on the end product than on the process of getting there.

During setup of governance infrastructure, if not done already at the portfolio level, the steering group will evaluate all proposals for projects. They will choose those proposals most closely aligned with corporate strategy and most feasible within the existing constraints (resources, time, budget, capital outlay for specialized equipment and so on).

Project goals
When *setting the goals for a project* the steering group defines:

- The desired business benefits and the measures and tolerances to be used to determine if they have been attained.
- The project deliverables required to achieve the business benefits, including the products or services the project has to deliver.
- The project success criteria with measures and tolerances to be used.

Also, the steering group will agree on the project management process required to achieve these objectives with the project manager.

The project management process can be expected to differ on the basis of the underlying governance paradigm.

Steering groups working within an outcome oriented governance paradigm (Flexible Economist and Versatile Artist) will typically develop a project charter. This document will include, along with other mandated guidelines, the sequence of deliverables and prioritization of functions to be developed. The project charter becomes the basis for the project team to use when developing the project plan.

Behaviour oriented paradigms shift parts of the responsibility for developing the project plan to the steering group. Examples for that are agile project management methods, which force the project sponsor (that is, the Steering Group) to define, prioritize and sequence incrementally the functions or features to be developed, so that the project team can focus almost entirely on the technical development process.

Means to achieve project goals
When providing the means to achieve the project goals the steering group performs governance and support roles in parallel.

The *governance role* is carried out through provision of various resources in accordance with the latest project plan (including any deviations or changes to the baseline plan). The types of resources provided can include, but are not limited to:

- people and skill sets;
- budgets;
- training and consulting;
- technical and communication infrastructures.

A pivotal resource is provided by designating who will be the project manager.

The *support role* includes activities to anchor the project within the organization. This involves:

- working on removing obstacles;
- reducing risks arising from the relationship between parent organization and project;
- linking project and organizational success factors;
- mitigating the impact of resource shortages, shortfalls on project results or business benefits.

Similar to managers of programs and portfolios, managers in the steering groups work to continuously improve their organization's project delivery capability. This is done through improvement of organizational processes, improvements in skill set, resource availability and general improvements in efficiency.

Progress control
These roles address both the details of the project, project context and environment. The following are continuously monitored and adjustments made as and when appropriate:

- project progress;
- achieved results;
- critical success factors;
- stakeholder interest.

Formal measurement of the above is set up, consisting of quality indicators, milestone and other achievements and general plan adherence. These measures are formally evaluated, quantified wherever possible and become input for performance assessments and project forecasts.

From a broader perspective, the *progress control* role of the steering group includes, among others, the prevention of scope creep and the management of contingency reserves.

Steering group meetings
These meetings are initiated at the start of the project. They are typically held more frequently in the first few phases and last few phases of a project, when they might be held weekly or, on high profile projects, even more frequently. During the other project phases they will usually be held monthly and at agreed-to decision points, such as Stage Gate or Toll Gate reviews.

GOVERNANCE VIEWS

Above we discussed what the roles of governance are. The following shows how these roles are applied to the governance of projects. For that the project is viewed as:

- The transaction to be performed, which is the project as an object consisting of contract, process, method and outcome.
- The agency performing the transaction, which is the project as an object consisting of the project manager and her team.

Governance of the project as a transaction

In Chapter 1, I defined transactions as being the conversion of *input* to *output*, explained through TCE (Williamson 1975, 1985). Using this principle, decisions on how to govern the *project as a transaction* are made on the basis of keeping the costs of governance to a minimum. These are the costs of:

- *Adaptiveness*. The costs arising from the need to align the interests of the various parties involved in the contract. The contract needs to ensure an increase in collaboration and a decrease in the potential for opportunism of the various parties involved. Contract mechanisms often used for this purpose include incentives for suppliers, like a bonus payment for project delivery on or before a certain date, or at or below a certain cost.
- *Contract Governance*. The costs involved in governing contract execution, including the costs of monitoring and control of project execution in accordance with the contract. Also included are the costs of steering group meetings and Stage Gate Reviews.
- *Contract Administration*. The costs for developing and agreeing on the contract contents. This includes not just the contractual terms, but also the costs of agreeing on the scope of the project and its objectives, as well as governance processes, such those for change management or reporting.

There are several factors taken into account when deciding on how best to minimize the above costs. These are:

1. The uniqueness of the product (that is, asset specificity).
2. The risk of the endeavor (that is, uncertainty).
3. The extent to which the endeavor is a one-time undertaking or can be repeated (that is, frequency).

Winch (2001) described these three factors as the space within which the project process is governed. He pointed out that none of them in isolation pose an undue risk to the project; it is only in their interaction that they become troublesome.

For example, by removing uncertainty it would be possible to write complete and all inclusive contracts to negate opportunistic behaviour arising from asset specificity.

The individual degree to which these three factors predominate and are combined in any given project influences its governance structure.

Contract development

Through their governance role of *setting goals*, steering groups carry out the work of contract administration. A contract is a promise or set of promises between parties, which the law will enforce. It is an instrument for balancing risk, with the distribution of risks between contract partners impacting the motivation to manage the specific risks for which each partner is responsible. (Dingle et al. 1995).

Work on the contract starts long before the contract enters negotiation. It begins with development and agreement on the project's business case. The sponsor or steering group must ensure development and acceptance of the business case within the organization. The business case is an assessment of the extent to which a project is expected to contribute to the organization's strategic objectives and constitutes the justification for the project. If the project's contribution is to the corporate strategic objective of cost reduction, (for example, through a new IT system), then the business case will need to examine the impact of the project outcome with cost reduction in mind. In its various roles for control, the steering group assesses the project outcome against the business case in order to decide on project feasibility contrasted against the financial impact on the business.

The next step is to develop a project charter or statement of work for the project. This document is owned by the sponsor or steering group and, at least the initial draft, will be developed by them. It defines the project scope and possible constraints in implementation. It is also the basis for project contract negotiations and for the project team to develop a preliminary project plan.

Following TCE principles the contract type should be selected based on who controls the risk (Müller and Turner 2005, Turner 2004), for example, if:

- The project manager (supplier) controls the risk. The ideal contract type is a fixed-price contract, preferably including functional specifications. The underlying assumption for this type of contract is that the major risk is how the project delivery process is managed and the steering group can make no contribution to solving the delivery problem.
- The sponsor (buyer) controls the risk. In cases of low complexity re-measurement contracts (for example, time and material contracts) are usually used. In cases of high complexity a cost-plus-incentive-fee contract type is usually used. The underlying assumption is that the major risk lies

in the definition or design of the product that the project is set up to deliver. The steering group or sponsor will be the participant who contracts out the work of product delivery and they can be expected to be the SME (Subject Matter Expert) most capable of assessing risk in product design.

- Both control the risk. Appropriate contract type is an alliance. The project comprises the steering group and the contractor as almost equal partners. Alliance contracts need to be carefully managed, with all parties kept informed of progress and involved in decision making.

The type of contract chosen influences both the governance structure itself and the rigor and depth of its implementation. Some of the possible risk stemming from the different contract types and their associated governance are:

- Fixed price contracts tend to lower governance efforts as the risk is on the side of the supplier and the price is fixed for the buyer.
- Re-measurement contracts typically involve more governance efforts than fixed price contracts as the sponsor or steering group has to ensure that their money is spent wisely.
- Alliance contracts involve the greatest amount of governance, as the relationships between buyer and seller are often complex and ambiguous.

As part of their work in governance of the contract the steering group and the project manager must agree how to:

a) Make mutually agreed adaptations to the contract to meet any unforeseen circumstances if and when they occur.
b) Communicate with each other to identify when such circumstances require a contract modification and to agree which detailed adaptation will be required.

Once a contract is in place, which specifies the objectives and deliverables of the project, the next task of the steering group is to agree, together with the project manager, the type of project management methodology to be applied. The choice of methodology determines, among other factors, the processes for project management, risk and change management. It also determines which associated templates, tools and techniques are to be used. A classification of methodologies undertaken by The Stationary Office (2008) grouped them into predictive, convergent and emergent methodologies:

- *Predictive Methodologies.* These are the traditional project management methodologies, for example, PRINCE2 (CCTA 2000) or PROPS (Ericsson 1999). The main characteristic of this type of methodology is that it is based on a linear process model, which is often sequential and not iterative in nature. This requires complete planning of the project before, or very shortly after, the productive work begins. This type of methodology was developed mainly to cater for projects with deliverables that can only be used when the project has been completed in its entirety, that is, when all project phases have delivered all of the components of the product. Examples are construction projects for bridges and manufacturing projects for cars. This type of methodology is also preferred to support fixed price/ fixed date contracts.

- *Convergent Methodologies*. An example is DSDM (Dynamic Systems Development Methods). The main characteristic of this type of methodology is that little planning is done upfront and only then at a moderate level of detail. This type of methodology supports projects where the details of the deliverables cannot be clearly defined at the start.
- *Emergent Methodologies*. Examples are Extreme Programming or Scrum. The main characteristic of this type of methodology is to allow for incremental building of the project deliverables. Product core functionality is developed first and is placed into productive use while the next phases of the project are ongoing, developing enhanced product functions in parallel. The advantage of this type of methodology is that benefits are initially created and can be used at the early stages of the project and enhanced benefits follow at the completion of each project phase. The impact is that the sponsor and steering group are required to have an in-depth understanding of project requirements and priorities.

The choice of methodology depends on project type and the nature of the project deliverable. The methodology chosen has an impact on governance of that project, as it defines both the relationship between project manager and steering group and the type of information exchanged during steering group and other governance and project meetings.

The final task of the steering group is to define the mechanism for assessing how well the completed project met its original objectives.

Progress control

In their role of *controlling progress* the Steering Group performs contract governance. They assess compliance with the contract by reviewing and evaluating the plan, process and performance of the project, as well as the level of achievement in relation to the project plan. This is typically done through formal reviews at predetermined points in the project process, normally at the end of project phases, or the implementation of major deliverables. Depending upon the methodology used these reviews are known variously as Tollgate Reviews (Ericsson 1999), Stage Gates Review (Cooper, Edgett and Kleinschmidt 2000) or Gateway Reviews (OGC 2008). Table 5.1 shows the OGC recommendations as an example.

Table 5.1   Gateway recommendations (OGC 2008)

Gateway	Phase	When done
Gateway 0 review	Strategic assessment	Done to initiate a project
Gateway 1 review	Business justification	Done after the business case has been developed
Gateway 2 review	Delivery strategy	Done after development of the project plan and assessment of the feasibility of goal achievement
Gateway 3 review	Investment decision	Done after procurement plans and/or project teams have been determined
Gateway 4 review	Readiness for service	Done after project deliverable(s) have been created
Gateway 5 review	Operational review and benefits realization	Done after project deliverable(s) is/are in productive use and the project benefits should have been realized

At each of these Gateways the project risks, project context and infrastructure, lessons learned, documentation, progress and status of the project are assessed to decide on continuation, change or suspension of the project or the resources provided to it.

Means to achieve project goals
Through their role of *providing the means to achieve project objectives* the steering group provides the means for contract adoption by the various parties to it.

From a contracting perspective this includes the contractual incentives for performance in delivery of the project and alignment of the objectives of the various stakeholders. From a governance perspective this includes provision of facilities, resources, decisions and budgets by the steering group to enable the project team to do its work. From a support perspective it includes the adoption of the project by the parent organization by establishing the framework for the project deliverables to be accepted and the project to be successful.

This section discussed governance of the project as a transaction. There is, however, another view of the project. This is the agency, or temporary organization, which also needs to be governed – the topic of the next section.

Governance of the project as an agency

Beside process and contract there is the human part of the project which also needs to be governed. In Chapter 2 I discussed the project as an agency for managing uncertainty, change and resource utilization. How is this agency linked to and managed in the parent organization?

For the project to be viable it must align to the business, the parent and the project organizations.

Alignment to business
Alignment of the *project to the company's business* is done through the strategic alignment described earlier, but also through the organization of projects as part of the company business. Turner and Keegan (2001) found that project-based organizations organize their governance processes differently depending on whether their clients are small or large and whether the projects for these clients are small or large. These are presented below:

- *Large projects for large clients* are setup as projects in a traditional sense, with dedicated teams and command and control structures specific to this temporary organization. Team structures are continuously changing to fit the needs of the project and its tasks. Governance in these projects is often done through direct contact between the project manager as supplier and the sponsor / steering group as buyer.
- *Many small projects for large clients* are often done by homogeneous teams, responsible for their own projects from beginning to end, but guided by an overall program manager. Communication with each client is channeled through the program manager. This ensures a coherent understanding of the contribution that all of these small projects make to the client's business. The program manager becomes the sponsor and governs the projects for that particular client.
- *Many small projects for many small clients* are typically staffed from a common resource pool. Turner and Keegan's investigation identified two distinct roles. These roles are the broker and the steward. The broker is an extrovert, entrepreneurial type, maybe a program manager, who builds and maintains the relationship with the client. The steward is a more introverted role, maybe a portfolio manager, who puts together the network of resources to deliver the project. The steward ensures availability of the right person at the right place and time, taking into account the long term objectives of the client and interaction with other projects and their resource needs. The project manager manages the process to deliver the project. Governance of project is undertaken by the broker, or program manager, on behalf of several clients.

- *Large projects for many clients* are often for small or startup companies with a very small set of products (or even just a single product), which are always tailored to the individual needs of the customer. Effectively delivering the product is a large project and the project teams work on different versions of the product tailored to each customer. Governance is the responsibility of the technology head of the product as the best resource to govern product development.

These categories have implications for governance. Only in the case of large projects for large or many clients do we see direct project governance by the sponsor. In the other cases governance is undertaken indirectly, with a broker, maybe in the form of a program manager, who acts as a go-between for the project sponsor and the project manager. The broker acts as an intermediate governance institution (steering group) for the project and as project representative for the sponsor. This has implications for communication between the project and its governance institution, which are addressed later in this chapter.

The alignment between parent organization and the project as an agency is discussed in the following.

Alignment of parent and project organization
This is done through governance of the link between the functional and the project organization. The link is prone to potential conflicts. In our work on the nature of the temporary organization Rodney Turner and I (Turner and Müller 2003) outlined the three perspectives the permanent organization has towards the project:

1. *An agency for change*: Projects and their teams are put in place to establish a beneficial change. However, people in the traditional, functional organization do not like change. Research has shown repeatedly that people in the traditional functional, permanent, organization are resistant to change. Unfortunately, the project exists with *the precise purpose* of bringing about change! The best way to manage this area of potential conflict is to ensure that it is governed through careful preparation of the permanent organization for the upcoming change, preferably supported by an appropriate incentive system.
2. *An agency for resource utilization*: In project-based organizations the permanent organization assigns their resources to projects. This results in productive use of those resources and they contribute to the functional manager's percentage resource utilization objectives. However, instead of harmony, this brings up a major conflict of interests between the functional manager and the project manager. The functional manager would like her resources to be assigned to projects for as long as possible, so that they can maximize their productive hours. On the contrary, the project manager would like the resources only to work and report time for those hours a resource is planned to work on the project. If the resource spends more time

than planned working on a project the project cost objectives are at risk. From the functional manager's perspective however, if the resource spends only a portion of their time (for example, 5 hours a day) on the project it may be difficult to assign the balance of their time to other projects, posing a risk to resource productivity goals. This conflict of interests is one of the reasons why the roles of line manager and project manager are incompatible and are difficult to be effectively combined in one person. Again, this conflict of interests is best governed by a farsighted and multi-dimensional incentive system.

3. *An agency for managing risk*: The project form of organization is currently the best way of minimizing the risk in executing unique, transient and novel endeavors. The perspective of the project as an agency for managing risk has the least potential for conflict. However, there have been a few interesting developments in recent years. One of them is spectacularly illustrated by a company approach of:

> *Everything we do is a project. Even measuring our achievements against the annual plan (including production) is a project.*

This is typical of managers of organizations that have switched to a high percentage of project-based work. They have become very impressed by the productivity gains and speed of change inherent in the project way of working. In their attempt to maximize these benefits for the entire organization the temptation has been to extend the project way of working beyond the boundaries of the traditional project. They extend the definition of the project as a novel, unique and transient undertaking but unfortunately ignore two major implications of project work that are unavoidable:

- Projects incur additional costs when compared to the non project work of the functional organization. These are the costs for establishing additional control structures and the costs of mitigating the information imbalance between project manager and governance institution. The nature of these costs is unique for each project. They are known as agency costs (Müller and Turner 2005).
- Not all people like or have the disposition to do project-based work. Project work, by its very nature, results in a higher level of employee stress compared to traditional work. Deadlines, time and cost constraints, constant changing of work locations and so on – all an inevitable part and parcel of the project way of working – become additional stress factors. Research by Turner et al. (2008) showed that working in projects is a self-selected career. Some people like the additional stimuli of project work and select the project as the cornerstone for their career. Others perceive these pressures as unwelcome and unwanted additional stress factors and prefer a career in the functional organization.

Going overboard and using the project as a vehicle for almost everything can therefore lead both to inefficiencies and, even worse, potential loss of those scarce and otherwise valuable resources that are unsuited to project work. Therefore it is unwise to view the project way of working as a panacea universally suitable for all endeavors. As a means to accomplish organizational results, it should be limited to only those endeavors that carry sufficient risk to warrant taking on board the inherent implications as outlined above. The corporation is best advised to evaluate all factors very carefully, both positive and constraints, when making the decision whether an endeavor is better done by the traditional functional organization or by the project organization.

Rodney Turner and I (Turner and Müller 2003) also said the *Project Manager should act as the Chief Executive Officer (CEO) of the project as an agency for change.* Project Managers are responsible for project results and accomplishment of objectives. They have to accomplish their plans by getting required resources when needed for the project. The danger is that these project managers become too 'my project' focused and insufficiently focused on the greater good of the organization as a whole. Project managers who become dominating and insist on getting resources exactly when *they* need them (maybe because they work on a high priority project) can take resources away from projects that, from the overall organization perspective, have a higher value at that particular time. This constitutes a high risk of compromising organizational efficiency and will often cause an overall performance risk.

A solution might be found in a remuneration system for project managers that rewards not just individual project results but also the results of the wider organization. Just as the CEO of the company should make decisions based on what is best for the entire company and not just individual departments, so the CEO of the project needs to balance a number of conflicting objectives to ensure the best results for the entire stakeholder community and not just individual projects.

CONCLUSION

This section has shown some possible conflicts arising from how to effectively link the permanent and the temporary organization. Governance of this link requires good communication structures and the establishment of mutual understanding between the two organizations in order to develop the best solution in each particular project setting.

Overall, a remuneration system is suggested that rewards managers' thinking beyond the boundaries of their own particular organization. Functional managers should be rewarded not just for achieving the objectives of their own organization but also be rewarded for supporting project work and project results. Similarly, project managers should be rewarded not only for their own projects results, but also for the contributions they make to achieve the objectives of the permanent organization.

A growing number of organizations reward project managers on the basis of performance in their own projects. However, fewer organizations factor in project results to the remuneration of their functional managers. This is certainly an area in need of further development.

How much governance is enough?

So far we have established the need for governance of the project-based part of the organization. The need for governance is clear; this is not a luxury to be avoided when budgets are tight. However, how much governance is needed? Can one have too little governance – or too much? This section deals with the question of what constitutes the optimum level of governance.

One of the key dimensions of governance is the quantity and style of collaboration between the steering group and the project manager. My 2003 research (Müller 2003), carried out on more than 200 projects worldwide, identified a two-dimensional model of steering group – project manager governance (see Figure 5.1, below).

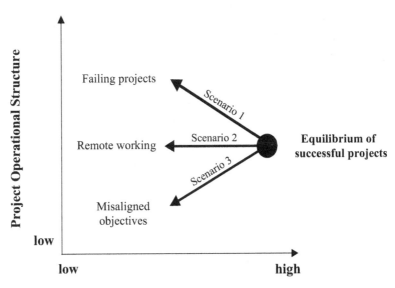

Steering Group – Project Manager Collaboration

Figure 5.1   Governance equilibrium and its deviations

The dimensions of the figure above are:

- *Steering Group – Project Manager Collaboration*: Collaboration between steering group and manager. This dimension is determined by:
  - The clearness of project objectives. The clearer they are for both project manager and steering group the higher the chances for project success.
  - The relational norms between the steering group and the project manager. That is the extent of both parties' flexibility (willingness to make adaptations), solidarity (avoidance of behaviour detrimental to the relationship) and willingness for information exchange (proactive, frequent sharing of information). The higher they score in these measures the more successful are the projects and their governance.
- *Project Operational Structure*: The level of structure the steering group imposes on the project manager. That is, the level of formality and reporting that is required and the extent to which the steering group expects the project manager to follow the mandated project methodology rigorously and inflexibly.

The research concluded that well governed projects cluster around the highest levels of collaboration and medium levels of operational structure. This means:

- Both parties are highly flexible and interested in a mutual partnership. The value they attach to their joint goals of the project may be higher than the value they attach to the goals of their respective parent organization. This enables high collaboration through open communication, mutual understanding of perspectives and a shared understanding of the project goals.
- The level of structure is held at a medium level. In practice that means the minimum level necessary, both in terms of the organizational structure of the parent organization and the level of operational reporting and other overhead tasks that are enforced through strict compliance with a project methodology. Sufficient freedom and authority is given to the project manager to solve day-to-day issues without involvement of the steering group.

The operational structures should be lowered to the point that the project manager has sufficient freedom to manage the project and the steering group feels comfortable with the amount, quality and frequency of information from the project. This equilibrium then allows for lowest communication costs, achieved through high collaboration and medium structure. Project costs can therefore be minimized, among others, through appropriate investment in communication structures. Increasing efforts in communication up to the point of governance equilibrium leads to reduction of administrative costs in projects. Increase of communication efforts over and above this point increases administrative costs unnecessarily. An effect described in scenario 1 below.

Failing projects often show an increase in reporting and other overhead tasks above the equilibrium point of high collaboration and medium structure. This is explained with the following three scenarios, as shown in Figure 5.1. Starting from the equilibrium point of governance, high performing projects with high collaboration and medium structure, we follow the three paths of imperfection shown in the figure:

Scenario 1 – Failing projects leading to increased control and structure
This happens if the project gets into difficulty. There is a loss of trust in the project manager's competence and the processes he or she is using. The steering group may decide to replace the project manager, but the legacy of distrust means they now impose a higher degree of structure and more frequent reporting and other overhead tasks in an attempt to avoid the problem reoccurring. This may lead to a stifling of productive work due to inflexibility and an excessive number of hours spent on overhead tasks.

Scenario 2 – Remote working leading to falling collaboration
This happens in virtual relationships over large geographical distances. The parties try to save costs by minimizing face-to-face communication (tele/video conferences and physical travel) with each other. This is often triggered by a misunderstood *management by exception* approach of the steering group. In an effort to reduce costs the parties agree that they only want communication about anything endangering the project and major milestones. Often the parties misunderstand this to mean that, outside of major formal reviews, only crisis level communication is necessary. Communication between the parties is reduced to below the necessary minimum. This may lead to a loss of clarity of objectives and a loss of effective working relationships, causing a failing project.

Scenario 3 – Misaligned objectives through informal reporting
This happens when informal and infrequent communication predominates heavily over formal communication, for example at stage gate reviews. Communication is typically by non documented phone calls and by chance face-to-face meetings (the infamous 'water cooler' meetings). The result is the lack of a vehicle for the steering group to govern the project. As a consequence, the steering group's objectives become misaligned from what the project manager is doing and the project manager loses sight of what the steering group wants. This leads to failing projects and potential replacement of the project manager, associated with a switch to scenario 1.

Agency Theory, as described in Chapter 1, tells us that these problems occur through information imbalance. The steering group knows less about the status of a project than the project manager and is uncertain whether the project manager is always acting in their best interest. This conflict is solved by an effective exchange of information. Both the steering group and the project manager have legitimate information requirements from each other.

Questions the steering group wants the project manager to answer are (Graham 2003):

- Will the end deliverable meet our functional requirements?
- Is the right project process being followed and will it successfully deliver the required deliverables in the optimum way?
- Will the project meet the required quality, budget and schedule requirements?
- Are there appropriate control mechanisms in place to achieve the above?
- Can we be sure that the project manager will always behave in a professional and trustworthy manner?

The project manager's information requirements change over the life-cycle of the project:

- At the early stages, the project manager needs to know the steering group's actual requirements and the context of the project. Both are needed to develop the project's 'big picture', which then becomes the base for decisions made during the project.
- During the planning phase, information about project objectives, specifications, priorities and possible constraints are needed.
- There is a big change in communication needs during the implementation stage of the project. The steering group extends from being information provider to becoming information receiver. The steering group reviews and formally accepts plans, changes and deliverables and expects the project manager to issue an early warning if the project is endangered. The steering group needs to be certain the project can fulfill its business obligations as stated in the project plan.
- At the project close-out phase, the steering group again becomes information provider, delivering information about the degree to which the project achieved its overall business objective. That information allows the project manager to deduce lessons learned for future projects and provide adequate information to the project team and other stakeholders.

The depth of information each party is looking for is heavily influenced by the type of contract chosen. The party controlling the risk is motivated to communicate. Any gap between the contractually mandated communication and actual communication needs as outlined above can have severe implications on the ability to govern the project. These implications differ by contract type.

Using the model of Figure 5.1 we find that the two negative scenarios occur when the contract type shifts all the risks to only one of the contractual parties. The types that do this are fixed price and time and materials contracts.

1. Fixed price contracts encourage developments found in scenario 2. All the risks are shifted to the project manager. The steering group has no direct need to follow up on project status. The steering group assumes that the project is proceeding according to plan as long as they have not been made aware of any plan deviations. The steering group's interest and involvement in the project decreases which leads to an information imbalance about status and possible risks. In Chapter 3 this was identified as being associated with low performing projects. The lack of steering group interest leads to lower collaboration, which, in turn, causes both parties to develop misaligned objectives, which, in turn, leads to lower project performance. Fixed price contracts tempt *steering groups* to neglect their professional obligations to the project and so threaten project success.
2. Time and material contracts encourage misalignment of objectives as found in scenario 3. The project manager and her team are paid simply for their effort (hours worked etc.) and not for achieving project objectives. Therefore the risk is assumed entirely by the steering group. The project manager has no direct incentive to adequately inform the steering group about project matters. Worse, the project manager might be tempted to compromise the time and performance objectives of the project, dragging it out unnecessarily, in order to maximize the financial results for her own company. Time and materials contracts tempt *project managers* to neglect their professional obligations to the project and so threaten project success.

So what can be done about it? Effective communication is the key.

These risks can be lowered through appropriate communication schedules, aiming for a balance between formal and informal communication with regular (weekly) meetings and monthly reports. These practices should be established between the parties, even if not mandated by contract. Appropriate and effective communication builds up the required collaboration and trust that allows the steering group to keep the level of formal structure of the project to a point where the project manager is empowered and has an adequate level of autonomy. The equilibrium of high collaboration but medium structure is reached.

Now that we have addressed the question of how much governance is needed, next we need to address how to choose an appropriate project manager.

CHOOSING AN APPROPRIATE PROJECT MANAGER

There is no *one size fits all* when it comes to project managers. Just as people come in all shapes and sizes, backgrounds and cultures so project managers have many varied and differing personalities.

Successful project managers need managerial competences that allow them to guide a team towards defined objectives. Managerial competences allow them to do things right. Many of these competences are described in this book. A long standing debate is also the level of technical competence a project manager should have. This depends on the project size, industry and complexity. *The Tasmanian Government Project Management Guidelines* (Tasmanian Government 2005, p. 19) suggest:

> *For large and/or complex projects, project management knowledge and experience are at least as important as knowledge of the business area(s) in which the project is being run. However, Project Managers should have, or seek to obtain, knowledge of the business area, in order to be able to communicate effectively with Project Team members and project clients to ensure that business issues and concerns are addressed.*

At the same time project managers need leadership competences, which allow them to *do the right things*.

In a worldwide study with almost 1000 participants Rodney Turner and I investigated the suitability of different project managers' intellectual (IQ), emotional (EQ) and managerial (MQ) capabilities for leadership in various project types and the impact these personality types had on the success of their projects (Turner and Müller 2006, Müller and Turner 2007). We found that emotional competency (EQ) of project managers correlates significantly with project success in high-performing projects of almost all types; the higher the EQ, the higher the level of project success.

At the detailed level we found that different kinds of projects require different competencies.

- Engineering and construction projects:
    - *Conscientiousness*: showing clear commitment to a course of action in the face of challenges and matching 'words and deeds' in encouraging others to support the chosen direction.
    - *Interpersonal sensitivity*: being aware of and taking into account, the needs and perceptions of others in arriving at decisions and proposing solutions to problems and challenges.

- *Engaging communication*: being approachable and accessible, engaging others and winning their support through an appropriate communication style for each audience.
- IT Projects:
  - *Engaging communication*, as above.
  - *Self-awareness*: being aware of their own feelings and being able to recognize them.
  - *Developing resources*: encouraging others to take on ever more demanding tasks, roles and accountabilities.
- Organizational Change Projects:
  - *Engaging communication*, as above.
  - *Motivation*: showing drive and energy to achieve clear results and make an impact.

We found that one competency, vision and imagination, correlates negatively with success in all types of high performing project. Visionary and imaginative people are without doubt important to project success, but when project managers are too imaginative they can compromise the task at hand. Conscientiousness is much more important to successful project management than vision. Vision and imagination are better supplied by people in other roles, for example, the project sponsor, who sets and communicates a project's objectives.

Steering groups should evaluate the specific leadership needs for each project and pay careful attention to matching project types with appropriate project managers. Not all candidate project managers will have the necessary competencies from the outset. However, a good project manager can be helped to develop the skills appropriate for the work they are doing.

SUMMARY

This chapter provided an overview of the breadth and depth of the steering group's role in the governance of projects. The next chapter combines the governance of project management, portfolio, programs and projects into a model for total governance of projects in organizations.

CHAPTER 6

TOWARDS AN INTEGRATED GOVERNANCE MODEL

The previous chapters presented the roles and tasks for governance of project, programs, portfolios and project management in an organization. This chapter links them all together into a comprehensive model.

The chapter starts from a practical perspective by looking at the link between the objectives of the different governance institutions and how that impacts the responsibilities, metrics for measurement of objective accomplishment, associated tools and organizational outcomes. This is followed by the theoretical perspective, which links the different governance theories into a model. Finally the different elements of the model are linked together using the project governance paradigm.

LINKING GOVERNANCE OF PROJECTS, PROGRAMS AND PORTFOLIOS

The previous chapters provided details of the governance function for projects, programs and portfolios. Now we look at the macro level to see how their respective roles are linked together in the context of the wider organization.

Table 6.1 gives an example of this linkage. As there is a huge variety of organizational structures, governance approaches and objectives not only based on industry, but also between different companies in the same industry, it is not possible to identify a one size fits all standard. Therefore only this example is given.

The responsibilities of the organizations are broken down hierarchically, as are the associated objectives and their metrics. Examples are given for possible tools and outcomes.

Table 6.1   Example of organizational linkage

Organization	Responsibility	Objectives	Metrics	Tools	Outcomes
Portfolio Mgt.	Selection and prioritization of projects and programs	Achievement of strategic objectives	Measures of strategic goal achievement	Profit and Loss / Utilization	List of prioritized projects / Resource requirements for line mgt.
Line Mgt.	Provide skills and resources for programs and projects	Organizations annual plan achievement	Budgets / Availability of skill sets / Staff development	Utilization reports / Resource database / Resource management tools	Skills available in sufficient quantity and quality
Steering Group	Achieving business case / Benefits creation / Project governance	Program and project success as contributor to business case	Business case measures / Planned benefits	Business case / Project/program status report / Governance policies	Resources in place / Governance and support for project/programs / Governance framework
Program Mgt.	Stakeholder management	Delivery of Benefits	Measures of How Well Benefits were Delivered	Electronic tools / Status reports	Stakeholder management / Benefits delivery
Project Mgt.	Delivery of project outcomes	Time, cost, quality plus other success factors	As specified in contract (for example, performance or specifications)	Electronic tools / Status reports	Project results as required
Strategic PMO	Improve effectiveness achieving strategic objectives	Portfolio optimization / Organizational project management maturity	Measures of corporate strategy / Maturity levels	Consolidated status reports and their analysis	Portfolio analysis and decision preparation for portfolio managers / Increasing organizational maturity
Tactical PMO	Control compliance with existing standards and best-practices / Train project managers	Supporting projects to become more efficient and effective / Train project managers	R-Y-G status of projects. / Percentage of 'red' projects against total number of projects / Organizational wide acceptance of methods and techniques	Project and program management methods, techniques and tools	Applied best-practices in projects / Better project results

A MODEL FOR GOVERNANCE OF PROJECTS, PROGRAMS AND PORTFOLIOS

A typical prerequisite for the model is a governance paradigm that defines the corporate perspective in relation to project management needs. The paradigm may vary by the different organizations within the corporation due to:

- A particular organization's specific objectives.
- The management culture instilled by the leaders of that organization.
- Contextual requirements when working with clients or networking with other firms.

Circumstances may cause organizations to override their default paradigm on a temporary basis, but they will return to default when these circumstances no longer apply. The default paradigm is often not communicated explicitly but set implicitly by the board of directors or other managers if delegated to them. The paradigm of choice (default or temporary) pervades the processes, policies and control mechanisms used by the corporation. It reflects the underlying assumptions about communication and interaction that takes place within the organization. The paradigm of choice determines how the organization can be governed.

The principal organizations in the governance model are the board of directors, steering group and PMOs. The principal governance hierarchy of, for example, a project, with its TCE and Agency Theory perspectives, is shown in Figure 6.1. Governance at each node in the hierarchy aims to accomplish its own objectives within the wider context of the organization. This is done by:

- Governing the 'transaction' of the next lower node by looking at the process and tasks they use to achieve their goals (contract).
- Governing the next lower node as an agency to accomplish change, utilize resources in the best possible way and minimize risks. This is done by aligning objectives and balancing information between the governing organization and its agency.

The above does not, however, explain acceptance of governance in the wider organizational and social context. To do this institutional theory is used, the third and final component of the theoretical model for governance of projects.

Institutional Theory

Institutional theory uses *legitimacy* to emphasize conformance with society and stakeholder values and expectations. It complements the primary determinants of organizational success; the rational perspectives of efficiency and effectiveness discussed so far and links governance to the more subjective aspects of

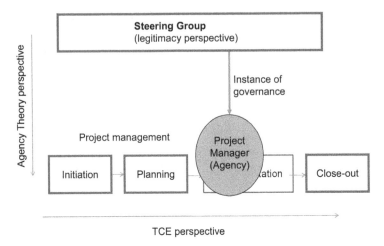

Figure 6.1   Model for project governance

management. Legitimacy aims to ensure that actions carried out and decisions taken during governance are performed in way that achieves legitimacy within its context. Legitimacy is defined as:

> *Legitimacy is a generalized perception or assumption that the actions of an entity are desirable, proper, or appropriate within some socially constructed system of norms, values, beliefs, and definitions.* (Suchman 1995)

Suchman (1995) describes legitimacy as a perception or assumption, which represents a reaction of the environment to the organization as they see it. Legitimacy reflects the extent of congruence between the behaviors of the legitimated entity (for example, the governance institutions) and the shared beliefs of some social group (for example, stakeholders and society-at-large).

By applying this concept to social enterprises Mason et al. (2007) conclude:

> *The outcome of an effective, ethical governance system is the achievement of legitimacy. Legitimacy enables us to frame (and measure) the appropriateness with which a [social] enterprise is governed. Furthermore, the governance system and processes must be repeatable over time, to continue meeting the needs of primary stakeholders, hence maintaining legitimacy. The ultimate aim for the [social] enterprise is long-term sustainability.*

Accordingly, organizations will need to seek legitimacy to justify their existence. Governance institutions achieve legitimacy by making decisions based on their legitimacy within a given context (society, company culture etc.).

Legitimacy is an umbrella term which is the combination of the three lower level specific forms of legitimacy (Suchman 1995) outlined below:

1. *Pragmatic Legitimacy* is based on self-interest and legitimizes actions that achieve highest benefit or utility in the eyes of the stakeholders or society in general.
2. *Moral Legitimacy* is based on ethical approval of actions. It legitimizes activities undertaken within the boundaries of the broader norms of society, no matter what the outcome may be.
3. *Cognitive Legitimacy* is based on comprehensibility and taken-for-grantedness. It legitimizes actions that are predictable, meaningful and self-evident by the perceiver.

Suchman (1995, referring to Scott and Meyer 1991) concludes that strong technical environments (such as technology companies) foster the need for pragmatic and moral legitimacy. Strong institutional environments (such as schools, churches and courts) favour *making sense* and *playing by the rules*, which fosters the need for cognitive and moral legitimacy even at the expense of their constituents.

Governance institutions therefore, will act and make decisions that balance benefit maximization, moral appropriateness and ease of understanding in the wider social or organizational context.

The model in Figure 6.2, summarizes the transaction, agency and legitimacy perspectives into a model for project governance. All components of the governance model are linked by a PMO to provide appropriate information flow through the organization.

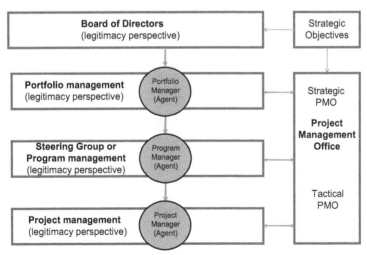

Figure 6.2   Project governance hierarchy

The transaction (TCE) perspective, as well as the agency perspective and their implications were discussed in Chapter 5.

The legitimacy perspective enables governance actions, including the project and its management, to gain social acceptance. Balancing pragmatic, moral and cognitive legitimacy for a given project context increases acceptance and 'social value' of a project. While this balance has the very real measurable benefit of reducing overhead costs, it also has the not insignificant 'soft' benefit of legitimizing the governance institution in the eye of the stakeholder and potentially society at large.

The total governance model

Finally the governance model for projects is complemented by the governance model for project management. The three steps of governance of project management (Chapter 3) can be seen as a third dimension, taking into account the timely development of project management within the organization.

The governance paradigm provides the link between governance of projects and governance of project management (Figure 6.3). A control paradigm such as the Conformist supports project management approaches as outlined in Step 1 of the three step governance model for project management. That is methodology compliance, audits and steering group observation. Contrarily, a Versatile Artist

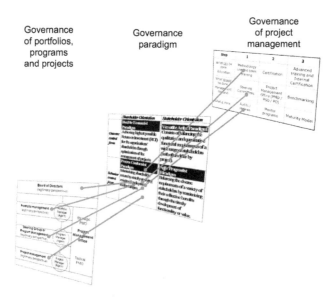

Figure 6.3   Governance model

paradigm will foster autonomy and trust in the project manager. By aligning the entire organization (for example, through the use of project management maturity models) to support the project-way-of-working the project manager has the flexibility and trust to balance requirements of various stakeholders.

Furthermore, the four governance paradigms tie together and categorize:

- the various ways of managing a project, given the implication stemming from TCE, agency theory and legitimacy;
- the corporate governance approach chosen, either primarily stakeholder or primarily shareholder oriented;
- the project management capabilities and practices deemed appropriate for all projects throughout the organization.

The paradigm influences the extent to which a corporation implements Steps 1–3 of the governance model for project management. It then synchronizes these project management capabilities with the level of control and autonomy needed for projects throughout the organization. It is the tool for linking capabilities with requirements in accordance with the wider corporate governance approach.

SUMMARY

The model developed in this chapter links existing theories to model the way projects and project management are governed in project-based organizations. It gives insight into the interaction between the different governance organizations, their roles and tasks, as well as the link to the project management skills and capabilities required to achieve governance objectives.

This chapter linked the contents of the former chapters into an overall model for governance of projects in a project-based organization. The next chapter looks at future developments in this area and summarizes the book.

CHAPTER 7

THE WAY FORWARD

THE WAY FORWARD

From observing the past history of governance and its current trends it is clear that governance was established to lower the risk for investors by reducing unethical conduct in organizations. The basis for doing this is transparency of the work of managers and the way business is conducted in organizations. Governance is driven further down the corporate hierarchy, from the board of directors, to the portfolio managers, program managers, steering groups and project managers.

Simultaneously, the sensitivity for ethical issues is on the rise within society. For example, the growing concern for others has led to a wide coverage of *Fair Trade* products. Hassel (2007) showed how the ethical conduct of business is reflected in a company's share price.

It is foreseeable that governance will be even more driven by ethical issues in the future. The relationship of a governance institution with its governed organization and stakeholders will increasingly have to address concerns for the environment, cultural diversity and ethical matters surrounding project outcomes and processes. Thus one objective of governance at all levels will be to provide a balance between what *could be done* and what *should be done* in the organization in order to ensure long term sustainability. Ethics, governance and sustainability will grow closer together.

Seen globally this indicates a growing importance of moral and cognitive legitimacy and a relative decline in pragmatic legitimacy. Within this global view exist many local variations and the decisions to be made in organizations and their projects will be subject to both global and many local influences – that is, the now well established 'glocal' mode of working. It will be interesting to watch the changes in goals, means to achieve these goals and control of progress in the coming years.

SUMMARY OF THIS BOOK

This book looked at the governance of project management, portfolios, programs and projects. It summarized the processes, roles and responsibilities of managers chartered with the governance of these organizations.

It started by introducing the shareholder and stakeholder theory, as well as TCE and agency theory as the theories underlying governance of organizations. By taking into account organization's preferences for project process or project outcome, four governance paradigms for the project driven part of the organization were developed. These paradigms were used throughout the book to explain the different preferences organizations have in goal setting for their projects and the related progress control techniques.

The principal institutions for governance of project and project management were introduced in Chapter 2 and their roles and responsibilities described. Chapter 3 presented the governance of project management within an organization as a three step model, from simple application of methods and audits, via PMOs to the use of project management maturity models. The model guides organizations in *how* and *why* they might develop their project management capabilities and to *what* extent.

Subsequently the governance of project portfolios and programs was presented, followed by the governance of projects. Here the processes, roles and activities were described. Agency theory and TCE provided the background to describe the need for these activities. Hints on the identification of appropriate managers at the three levels of portfolio, program and project were given.

Finally, a theoretical model was developed, based on the well established theories of TCE, Agency Theory and Institutional Theory. These theories explain the *why*, *how* and *when* in governance at the different levels. By linking the theoretical model with existing governance standards and research results the '*what to do*' in governance was addressed.

The two aspects of governance of projects (incl. programs and portfolios) and governance of project management were linked through the paradigms of *how projects are to be managed* within an organization. The four most often used paradigms were identified as well as the need for the adoption and possibly modification, of one or a combination of these paradigms by the board of directors. That closes the link between governance of projects and governance of project management and shows the responsibility of the board of directors and other executive managers in setting the stage for good project management in their organization.

This book has linked existing governance theories and existing methods, standards, guidelines and research results into a single model for governance of project management, portfolios, programs and projects. As a relatively young field of research the knowledge in this area of governance is currently developing and further refinements or alternative models can be expected over the coming years. The book reflects the current understanding and provides guidance for governance in practice. However, not only a practical, but also a theoretical purpose was pursued with this book. It was written for the academically interested practitioner as well as for the practically interested academic, in an attempt to bridge these two worlds in the hope and expectation that they can learn a lot from each other.

REFERENCES

Adler, T.R., Scherer, R.F., Barton, S.L. and Katerberg, R. (1998), 'An Empirical Test of Transaction Cost Theory: Validating Contract Typology', *Journal of Applied Management Studies* 7:1, pp. 185–200.

Andersson, A. and Müller, R. (2007), 'Containing Transaction Costs in ERP Implementation Through Identification of Strategic Learning Projects', *Project Management Journal* 38:2, pp. 84–92.

APM (2004), *Directing Change: A Guide to Governance of Project Management*, Association for Project Management, High Wycombe, UK. www.apm.org.uk. Last access 7 July 2008.

Barney, J.B. and Hesterly, W. (1996), 'Organizational Economics: Understanding the Relationship between Organizations and Economic Analysis,' in *Handbook of Organization Studies*, S.R. Clegg, C. Hardy, and W.R. Nord (eds)., Sage Publications, London, UK, pp. 115–47.

Bergen, M., Dutta, S., and Walker, O.C. (1992), 'Agency Relationships in Marketing: A Review of the Implications and Applications of Agency and Related Theories', *Journal of Marketing* 56:3, p. 1.

Blomquist, T. and Müller, R. (2006), *Middle Managers in Program and Portfolio Management: Practice, Roles and Responsibilities* (Newton Square, Project Management Institute).

Brown, S. and Eisenhardt, K. M. (1997), 'The Art of Continuous Change: Linking Complexity Theory and Time-paced Evolution in Relentlessly Shifting Organizations', *Administrative Science Quarterly*, 42, pp. 1–34.

CCTA (2000), *Managing Successful Projects with PRINCE2* (Norwich, The Stationary Office).

Chiu, L.F. (2006), 'Critical Reflection: More Than Nuts and Bolts', *Action Research* 4:2, pp. 183–203.

Clarke, T. (2004), 'The Stakeholder Corporation: A Business Philosophy for the Information Age', in Clarke, (ed.), *Theories of Corporate Governance: The Philosophical Foundations of Corporate Governance* (London, Routledge), pp. 189–202.

Clegg, S.R. (1994), 'Weber and Foucault: Social Theory for the Study of Organizations', *Organization* 1:1, pp. 149-78.

Clegg, S.R., Pitsis, T.S., Rura-Polley, T., and Marosszeky, M. (2002), 'Governmentality Matters: Designing an Alliance Culture of Inter-organizational Collaboration for Managing Projects', *Organization Studies* 23:3, pp. 317–37.

Cooper, J.M., Edgett, S.J., and Kleinschmidt, E.J. (2000), 'New Problems, New Solutions: Making Portfolio Management More Effective', *Research Technology Management* 43:2, pp. 18–33.

Cooper, R.G., Edgett, S.J., and Kleinschmidt, E.J. (2004a), 'Benchmarking Best NPD Practices - I', *Research Technology Management* 47:1, pp. 31–43.

Cooper, R.G., Edgett, S.J., and Kleinschmidt, E.J. (2004b), 'Benchmarking Best NPD Practices - II', *Research Technology Management* 47:3, pp. 50–9.

Cooper, R.G., Edgett, S.J., and Kleinschmidt, E.J. (2004c), 'Benchmarking Best NPD Practices - III', *Research Technology Management* 47:6, pp. 43–55.

Crawford, L., Cooke-Davies, T., Hobbs, J.B., Labuschagne, L., Remington, K. and Chen. P. (2008), 'Governance and Support in the Sponsoring of Projects and Programs', *Project Management Journal* 39:S1, S43-S55.

Crawford, L. and Turner J.R. (2005), 'Project Governance and Maturities', in *Proceedings of the Austrian PM Days 2005, Projects and Maturities*, Vienna, Austria.

Dingle, J., Topping, D., and Watkinson, M. (1995), 'Procurement and Contract Strategy,' in J. R. Turner, (ed.), *The Commercial Project Manager* (Maidenhead, McGraw-Hill).

Englund, R. and Müller, R. (2005), 'Leading Change Towards Enterprise Project Management,' in Y. C. Shekar (ed.) *Enterprise Project Management – An Introduction* (Hyderabad: ICFAI University Press).

Ericsson (1999), PROPS: A General Model for Project Management in a Multiproject Organization (Karlstad: Ericsson Project Management Institute).

Graham, R. (2003), 'Managing Conflict, Persuasion and Negotiation', in Turner, J. R. (ed.), *People in Project Management* (Aldershot: Gower Publishing).

Hassel, L. (2007), 'Miljöarbete ger högre börsvärd', *Dagens Industri*, 20 November 2007.

Helm J, and Remington, K. (2005), 'Effective Project Sponsorship: An Evaluation of the Role of the Executive Sponsor in Complex Infrastructure Projects by Senior Managers', *Project Management Journal* 36:3, pp. 51–61.

Hobbs, B. and Aubry, M. (2007), 'A Multi-Phase Research Program Investigating Project Management Offices (PMOs): The Results of Phase 1', *Project Management Journal* 38:1, pp. 74–86.

Jensen, M.C. (2000), *A Theory of the Firm: Governance, Residual Claims, and Organizational Forms* (Cambridge: Harvard University Press).

Judgev, K. and Müller, R. (2005), 'A Retrospective Look at Our Evolving Understanding of Project Success', *Project Management Journal* 36:4, pp. 19–31.

Kendall, G.I. and Rollins, S.C. (2003), *Advanced Portfolio Management and the PMO* (Fort Lauderdale: J. Ross Publishing).

Klakegg, O.L., Williams, T., Magnussen, O.M., Glasspool, H. (2008), 'Governance Frameworks for Public Project Develoment and Estimation', *Project Management Journal* 30:Supplement, S27–S42.

Lemke, T. (2001), '"The Birth of Bio-politics": Michel Foucault's Lecture at the Collège de France on Neo-liberal Governmentality', *Economy and Society* 30:2, pp. 190–207.

Liu, L. and Yetton, P. (2007), 'The Contingent Effects on Project Performance of Conducting Project Reviews and Deploying Project Management Offices', *IEEE Transactions on Engineering Management* 54:4, pp. 789–99.

Mason, C., Kirkbride, J. and Bryde, D. (2007), 'From Stakeholders to Institutions: the Changing Face of Social Enterprise Governance Theory', *Management Decision* 45:2, pp. 284–301.

Müller, R. (2003), *Communication of IT Project Sponsors and Managers in Buyer-Seller Relationships* (Parkland, USA: Universal Publishers).

Müller, R., Martinsuo, M. and Blomquist, T. (2008), 'Project Portfolio Control and Portfolio Management Performance in Different Contexts', *Project Management Journal* 39:2.

Müller, R. and Stawicki, J. (2007), 'A Framework for Building Successful Project-Based Organizations', *Project Perspectives* 29:1, pp. 68–71.

Müller, R. and Turner, J.R. (2002), 'A Model and Gap-Analysis of Buyer – Seller Communications in IT Projects', in *Proceedings of the PM-Days Research Conference*, November 27–28, 2002, Vienna, Austria

Müller, R. and Turner, J.R. (2005), 'The Impact of Principal-Agent Relationship and Contract Type on Communication between Project Owner and Manager', *International Journal of Project Management* 23:5, pp. 398–403.

Müller, R. and Turner, J.R. (2007) 'Matching the Project Manager's Leadership Style to Project Type', *International Journal of Project Management* 25:1, pp. 21–32.

Niehaves, B., Klose, K., and Becker, J. (2006), 'Perspectives on IT Consulting Projects: The Case of ERP Implementation', *e-service Journal* 2006, pp. 5–26.

OECD (2004), 'OECD Principles of Corporate Governance'. www.oecd.org. Last access 2005-1-10.

OGC (2008), OGC Governance. http://www.ogc.gov.uk. Last access 2008-07-02.

Partington, D., Pellegrinelli, S., and Young, M. (2005), 'Attributes and Levels of Programme Management Competence: An Interpretive Study', *International Journal of Project Management* 23:2, pp. 87–95.

Pellegrinelli, S., Partington, D., and Young, M. (2003), 'Understanding and Assessing Programme Management Competence', *in Proceedings of PMI's Global Congress 2003 – Europe, May 2003, The Hague, The Netherlands.*

PMI (2003), *Organizational Project Management Maturity Model: Knowledge Foundation,* (Newtown Square: Project Management Institute).

PMI (2006a), *The Standard for Portfolio Management* (Newtown Square: Project Management Institute).

PMI (2006b), *The Standard for Program Management* (Newtown Square: Project Management Institute).

Pryke, S.D. (2005), 'Towards a Social Network Theory of Project Governance', *Construction Management and Economics* 23:9, pp. 927–39.

Scott, W.R. and Meyer, J.W. (1991), 'The Organization of Societal Sectors'. In Powell, W.W. and DiMaggio, P.J. (eds.), *The New Institutionalism in Organizational Analysis*, pp. 108–140 (Chicago: University of Chicago Press).

SEI (1993), *Capability Maturity Model for Software*, 1.1 edn (Pittsburgh : Software Engineering Institute).

Stoker, G. (1998), 'Governance as Theory: Five Propositions', *International Social Science Journal* 50:155, pp. 17–28.

Suchman, M.C. (1995), 'Managing Legitimacy: Strategic and Institutional Approaches', *Academy of Management Review* 20:3, pp. 571–610.

Tasmanian Government (2005), *Tasmanian Government Project Management Guidelines, Version 6.0,* http://www.egovernment.tas.gov.au/themes/project_management. Last access 2008-08-24.

The Stationary Office (2008), '*Method Spectrum Diagram*', http://www.best-management-practice.com/gempdf/Agile_Project_Management_Contents_and_Introduction.pdf, last access 2008-08-08.

Turner, J.R. (1998a), 'Projects for Shareholder Value: The Influence of Project Managers', *Proceedings of IRNOP III – 'The Nature and Role of Projects in the Next 20 Years: Research Issues and Problems',* Calgary, Alberta, July, 283–291.

Turner, J.R. (1998b), Projects for Shareholder Value: The Influence of Project Performance Parameters at Different Financial Ratios, *Project Management*, 4.

Turner, J.R. (2004), 'Farsighted Project Contract Management: Incomplete in its Entirety', *Construction Management and Economics* 2:1, pp. 75–83.

Turner, J.R. (2007), *Gower Handbook of Project Management*, 4th edition (Aldershot: Gower Publishing).

Turner, J.R. and Keegan, A. (2001), 'Mechanisms of Governance in the Project-based Organization: Roles of the Broker and Steward', *European Management Journal* 19:3, pp. 254–67.

Turner, J.R. and Müller, R. (2003), 'On The Nature of The Project as a Temporary Organization', *International Journal of Project Management*, 21:1, pp. 1–7.

Turner, J.R. and Müller, R. (2004), 'Communication and Co-operation on Projects Between the Project Owner as Principal and the Project Manager as Agent', *European Management Journal*, 22:3, pp. 327–36.

Turner, J.R. and Müller, R. (2006), *Choosing Appropriate Project Managers: Matching their Leadership Style to the Type of Project* (Newtown Square: Project Management Institute).

Turner, J.R., Huemann, M, and Keegan, A. (2008), *Human Resource Management in The Project -Oriented Organization* (Newtown Square: Project Management Institute).

Williamson, O.E. (1975), *Markets and Hierarchies: Analysis and Antitrust Implications* (New York: Collier Macmillan).

Williamson, O.E. (1985), *The Economic Institutions of Capitalism* (New York: The Free Press).

Winch, G.M. (2001), 'Governing the Project Process: A Conceptual Framework', *Construction Management and Economics* 19:8, pp. 799–808.

INDEX

FUNDAMENTALS OF PROJECT MANAGEMENT AND ADVANCES IN PROJECT MANAGEMENT SERIES

Project management has become a key competence for most organisations in the public and private sectors. Driven by recent business trends such as fewer management layers, greater flexibility, increasing geographical distribution and more project-based work, project management has grown beyond its roots in the construction, engineering and aerospace industries to transform the service, financial, computer, and general management sectors. In fact, a Fortune article rated project management as the number one career choice at the beginning of the 21st century.

Yet many organisations have struggled in applying the traditional models of project management to their new projects in the global environment. Project management offers a framework to help organisations to transform their mainstream operations and service performance. It is viewed as a way of organising for the future. Moreover, in an increasingly busy, stressful, and uncertain world it has become necessary to manage several projects successfully at the same time. According to some estimates the world annually spends well over $10 trillion (US) on projects. In the UK alone, more than £250 billion is spent on projects every year. Up to half of these projects fail! A major ingredient in the build-up leading to failure is often cited as the lack of adequate project management knowledge and experience.

Some organizations have responded to this situation by trying to improve the understanding and capability of their managers and employees who are introduced to projects, as well as their experienced project managers in an attempt to enhance their competence and capability in this area.

FUNDAMENTALS OF PROJECT MANAGEMENT

This series of short guides covers the key aspects of project management: Benefits Management; Business Case; Change Management; Cost Management; Financing; Governance; Leadership; Organization; Program Management; Progress Management/Earned Value; Planning; Quality Management; Risk Management; Scope; Scheduling; Sponsorship; Stakeholder Management; Value Management.

Each guide, as the series title suggests, aims to provide the fundamentals of the subject from a rigorous perspective and from a leading proponent of the subject.

Visit: www.gowerpublishing.com/fundamentalsofprojectmanagement for more information and a list of titles.

ADVANCES IN PROJECT MANAGEMENT

Advances in Project Management provides short, state of play, guides to the main aspects of the new emerging applications of project management including: maturity models, agile projects, extreme projects, six sigma and projects, human factors and leadership in projects, project governance, value management, virtual teams, project benefits.

Visit www.gowerpublishing.com/advancesinprojectmanagement for more information and a list of titles.

SERIES EDITOR

Professor Darren Dalcher is Director of the National Centre for Project Management, a Professor of Software Project Management at Middlesex University and Visiting Professor of Computer Science at the University of Iceland.

National Centre for Project Management, Middlesex University, College House, Trent Park, Bramley Road, London N14 4YZ United Kingdom email: ncpm@ mdx.ac.uk Phone: +44 (0)20 8411 2299 Fax no. +44 (0)20 8411 5133.